...and then I painted the garage

Getting the job you want
in the least amount of time.

Larry Finkelstein

HighTide
Publications, Inc.

Deltaville, Virginia

High Tide Publications, Inc.
1000 Bland Point
Deltaville, Virginia 23043
www.hightidepublications.com

First Edition

ISBIN: 978-1-945990-71-7

Table of Contents

Forward

"Call Larry."
When life throws us a curve ball, after a brief moment of confusion either my husband or I will utter those words. Can't decide whether to move to take a new job? Worried about a health issue? Need to reevaluate the work-life balance?
"Call Larry."

My husband has been friends with Lawrence Finkelstein for four decades, and I for three. We know that Larry cares about us, that he is a good listener, and that he can re-frame a crisis so that it becomes a manageable situation. These traits make for an excellent friend, and I am sure they are among the skills Larry brings into the relationships he has with clients who are entering the workforce or changing their careers.

I think it is important for readers of this book to know that its author practices what he preaches. Larry has navigated personal and professional transitions in his own life with courage and persistence. For instance, he created his own consulting company, and a person doesn't succeed in an enterprise like that without first embracing an uncertain mix of risk and opportunity.

Similarly, when Larry moved to a new city, he flourished there, in part by creating an activities Meet-up group that grew from 10 members to over 1,500. This group has helped create bonds of friendship in the community while also building support for local businesses.

I am only half joking when I suggest that Larry run for mayor someday. He still makes time in his life to connect with his creative side through painting (not a garage, but abstract art) and to relax by enjoying reading, movies, and exercising.

If you are facing one of life's transitions, you probably can't just "call Larry." But you can do the next best thing. You can read this book and complete the exercises in it. You will gain insight into your own strengths and preferences. You will find guidelines to help you along your own path to success.

Enjoy the read, and enjoy your journey.

Beverly Peterson, PhD

- 1 - Prepare

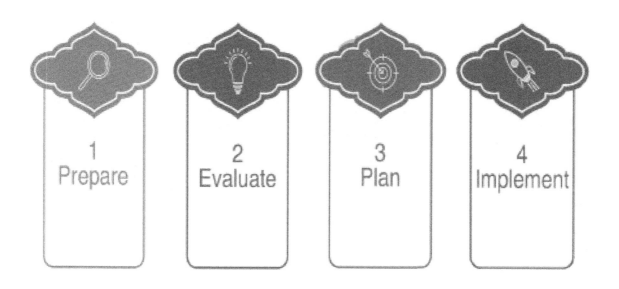

1 Prepare 2 Evaluate 3 Plan 4 Implement

What to Expect in this Section

Back in the Day

A lot has changed since I began doing career counseling. With management and professional level people, it was once a standard procedure to create a one-size-fits-all resume (or maybe two) and do a mass mailing as an important part of their job search.

Back in the day 100 or more resumes would be sent out at a time to potential employers. We would discuss with a client the texture of the paper to be used with the resume and the color (they had a choice of three). Mass mailings such as this never worked very well and would not be done now. First, when you contact an employer directly, you need to target them. How well do they fit the criteria the you have set as important to your career goals? Next, you would explore the possibility of personalizing any contact by networking into them using a third party's name (hopefully one the recipient knows well). Your resume would be tailored to a specific job and include "key words" that employer would be looking for. Because of the shift in technologies, most resumes are sent by email or as an attachment to a message.

Back in the day you would research a company in the library. While libraries are still useful, and may contain directories that you would otherwise have to pay for, most research is done on the Internet, often on the organization's home page. You can check out *Glassdoor* to see what previous employees thought of a company or what the pay is for different positions.

Back in the day want ads use to be found primarily in newspapers or other printed materials such as journals. Now, ads are found on broad based Internet sites or on the organization's home page. You want to use recruiters or agencies? The best way is to network into them, but this information can also be found on your computer. No longer do you have to find phone books in every area code where you may want to search.

The Preparation Phase

I realized, in the great majority of cases, spending a little more time in preparing for a job search would significantly reduce the time it would take to get the right position. Clients who spend the time for a thorough assessment, make a list of their accomplishments and transferable skills, and give thought to what they really want and the most effective way to reach their goals are the ones who reach these goals more quickly and with less frustration than those people who jump into their search with less preparation, an inadequate strategy, and a lack of clarity in their written marketing materials and interview techniques.

The investment of time searching for the right situation and prioritizing activities is small when compared with the positive outcome it provides. For example, using pertinent accomplishments in your resume or in explaining what you can do when networking has a positive impact on people. It is an excellent opportunity to share your achievements. The contributions you skip will often cost you money; the search will take longer, and you will be less impressive to your potential employer when it is time to negotiate the job. The same situation can occur when you fail to research the organizations you have an interest in working for. A well-prepared job applicant is impressive to an interviewer and, the more you know the better you will determine if the job is right for you.

The preparation phase includes more than what you are good at and would enjoy doing. It includes determining what is important to you in your life. It should answer such questions as:

- How do I determine what is important?

- How do I develop a balance among all these important elements?

- Can I have a great relationship, follow through on hobbies, develop myself as an individual, be a good parent (or child) and succeed at work?

- Do I have to sacrifice anything that is important? For how long?

- What will the sacrifice really cost me?

Being focused is significant for anyone thinking of a career transition. A lack of focus can come about for many reasons—the consequences are almost always the same. It hinders you in moving ahead in attaining your goals if you are unfocused. Your search will take longer, and it lessens the likelihood of job satisfaction.

So, what causes lack of focus?

Lack of focus can come from:

Poor self-esteem

Many people don't feel empowered to go after a job that will make them happy. Since their "self-talk" is negative they don't engage in the kinds of assertive communications that usually lead to success.

Fear of rejection following a job loss

Many people are reluctant in pursuing their goals after losing their job. I have worked with several high–level executives reluctant in setting goals or taking positive actions following a job loss. They had to deal with feelings of loss, depression and anxiety before they could move on. The experience of loss is often subjective; someone bases it on how you define things. Someone can be poor, have few economic resources, yet accept the loss of a position and immediately seek a new opportunity. Someone else, with a generous severance package and substantial savings, can go into a deep depression and take a long time to rebound.

Not wanting to rule out any options

There may be many things that an individual can do. In a desire to be considered for every option, some people may be vague about what they want to do or communicate too many options. This leads their contacts to conclude that they aren't focused. It is important to clarify what you want the most and to be specific to those from whom you are seeking help.

Lack of experience, access, or knowledge

Many people new to the workforce or have limited experience. Perhaps they were in one organization for the last 20 years, and have not kept up with a changing environment. Maybe they are unaware of viable options or have never learned the skills that lead to success. If they were never taught how to plan nor had a role model or mentor to guide them, they will be at a disadvantage in setting goals.

How Do You Make the Right Job Choice?

There are many factors in selecting the next position right for you, and this book will help you address them.

- What are your basic life goals and where do you see work fitting in?
- How much money do you need, or want, to make?
- How do you want to develop yourself?
- What do you want to learn about?
- What new skills do you want to gain?
- What kinds of relationships do you want to develop at work?
- What kind of boss do you get along with the best?
- Where can you find the best mentor?
- What are the opportunities for career growth?
- Which position provides you with the challenge you seek?
- Does the job provide you enough time to spend with family and friends?
- Will you be able to develop long-term economic security?

Job Search Quiz (Mark each one True or False)

This quiz tests your knowledge of job search techniques. The answers are on the following page.

1. The best way to get a job is through a headhunter	
2. Answering blind ads is a waste of time	
3. If you are over 40 you will have a hard time getting a job	
4. Temporary agencies focus only on clerical positions	
5. When asked to describe yourself in an interview you should try to do so in less than three minutes	
6. Most people underestimate their abilities	
7. A good resume is the most important part of your job search	
8. If you are not a perfect match you should not bother answering an ad	
9. It takes approximately one month of job search time to secure a position for every $10,000 you are looking for	
10. Most interviewers are competent and know precisely what they are looking for in a candidate	
11. A good resume can be as long as you want in order to list all the details of your background	
12. Discrimination regarding sex, race and age are a thing of the past	
13. You should always bring up salary at the beginning of an interview	
14. More organizations are using the Internet to get job candidates	
15. You should always ask permission before you smoke at an interview	
16. You should not bother family and friends regarding your job search	
17. After an interview, always wait for the employer to call you	
18. An employer can't make you take a pre-employment drug test	
19. Extroverts always have an easier time in getting a job	
20. Always take the first offer you get	

Answers to Job Search Quiz

1. The best way to get a job is through a headhunter? False.

While headhunters and employment agencies (including State Employment Services) can help in a job search, most jobs are filled through other means. Know that recruiters are looking to meet employers' needs with candidates who appear to be a good fit. They are especially not interested in people who want to change careers.

2. Answering blind ads is a waste of time? False.

Blind ads (those which do not identify the organization placing the ad) can be legitimate advertisements for employment. There are several reasons someone places that ad. The organization may not want a person about to be replaced to know of their decision or they may desire not to have to spend the time and money notifying applicants of the receipt or rejection of their resume. They sometimes use blind ads for trolling (seeing who is out there in case they want to hire).

3. If you are over 40 (or 50) you will have a hard time getting a job? Generally false.

While age discrimination continues to exist, it has transformed over time. First, being *washed-up* at 40 has been pushed back at least a decade (except for professional athletes who may be "over the hill" at 25 in some sports. There are several reasons for this. People get older later in both appearance and behavior.

The "baby boomers," a very significant segment of the population who are often in positions to hire, are getting older themselves. Employers realize that it is hard to get employees with great experience unless they have actually had the opportunity to live. There has been considerable legislation prohibiting age discrimination and successful litigation against employers who have discriminated in hiring and promotion. My experience is that the most important factor related to age in getting hired is your attitude towards yourself. The less it is an issue to you, the less it is an issue to others.

4. Temporary agencies focus only on clerical positions? False.

Temporary agencies have expanded the kinds of jobs they fill. There are now firms that specialize in various professional areas. Taking a temporary position can provide you with the opportunity to audition, to impress an employer enough they want to make you permanent.

5. When asked to describe yourself in an interview you should try to do so in less than three minutes. True.

Many people get nervous over having to answer the question - "Tell me about yourself." This is a great opportunity to provide an introduction to your background; don't assume that the person you are meeting has read or remembers your resume. They may interview several people for the position. Be concise. Give a brief history of your education, training, and experience as it relates to the job you are applying for.

6. Most people underestimate their abilities? True.

Most people forget what they had to learn to get to where they are. That is why it is important to review your skills and accomplishments before you interview. This is not bragging; it is taking responsibility for the contributions you have made.

7. A good resume is the most important part of your job search? False.

A good resume (an accurate representation of your background as it pertains to your employment goals) is very important but no more so than your ability to talk about yourself in positive terms as a solution to employer's problems.

8. If you are not a perfect match for a job you should not bother answering an ad? False.

When employers place an ad, they are starting a wish list. If you feel you can do the job, and are a fairly close match, reply. For instance, if they ask for 5 years experience, and you have only three, but you feel you can do the job, apply. Just ask yourself if there is any requirement in the ad that would prevent you from doing a job. Medical doctors need M.D.'s and truck drivers need a driver's license, so don't waste your time by applying for jobs for which you lack essential certifications.

9. It takes approximately one month of job search time to secure a position for every $10 thousand in salary you are looking for? False.

I spoke to the person who stated he was responsible for this statement (CEO of a major outplacement firm). He said he made up the figure when asked how long it takes to find a job. People always want to know how long their search will take. It depends on how marketable you are, how focused you are, how much effort you will put into the search, what the economy is like, and luck. Well-prepared, connected, hard–working people seem to be luckier.

10. Most interviewers are asked to describe competent and know precisely what they are looking for in a candidate? False.

Most of the people I have interviewed for this book have had little or no training in how to conduct an effective interview. Jack Cogger, a leading figure in the training of interviewers, estimated that only 15% of the people he met who did interviewing had received training.

11. A good resume can be as long as you want to list the details of your background? False.

A good resume should be one or two pages, determined by the amount of relevant experience. With those individuals who have published a great deal or hold several patents, you can create an addendum separate from the resume. The only exception is a curriculum vita (a special resume used by educators), which can often run many pages.

12. Discrimination regarding sex, race, and age are a thing of the past? False.

I believe the workplace is a slightly more level playing field than it was 30 years ago. People are more aware that what you can contribute is more important than gender, race or age. But the next time I meet someone who is free of all prejudices—well, it will be the first time.

13. You should always bring up salary at the beginning of an interview? False.

The interviewee (how's that for an awkward word) should not bring up salary. The interviewer will do so when ready. There is a general belief that the party who brings up money first has a slight disadvantage in negotiating.

14. More organizations are using the Internet to get job candidates? True.

The growth of organizations seeking job candidates on the Internet is astounding. There are now hundreds of sites advertising for workers, from organization's web pages, to freestanding job search sites like Monster.com and Indeed.com, to government run employment services. Sometimes employers are supplementing how they find new employees; with others, it has replaced older methods such as newspaper ads.

15. You should always ask permission before you smoke at an interview? False.

You should not smoke at an interview.

16. You should not bother family and friends regarding your job search? False.

You should seek networking assistance from people you know–including family and friends. It is amazing how many of your acquaintances have contacts that you may not be aware of. It will make them feel good if they can help, and it provides you with practical value.

17. After an interview, always wait for the employer to call you? False.

As the interview is ending ask the interview what the next steps of the hiring process are and determine when you can call to follow up. When you get home, immediately write a thank you note to the interviewer. Your thank you note is also an opportunity to highlight some of your strengths as related to the position.

> *Erin, the daughter of a friend, applied for a position with a country club. She interviewed for a position with a lot of competition. After much cajoling, we convinced her to send a thank you note. The organization was so impressed with her professionalism it offered her a better position that paid thousands more. Now, many years later, she holds a very significant position in a marketing firm and pays special attention to great customer service.*

18. An employer can't make you take a pre-employment drug test? False.

Yes, they can.

19. Extroverts always have an easier time in getting a job? False.

Most of your job search activities are developing self-knowledge, making one-to-one contacts for networking and interviews, and following through on telephone calls and written communications. Unless you are very shy, you can accomplish these activities.

20. Always take the first offer you get? False.

Unless you are desperate for money, take a position that meets most of your reasonable goals for a job. If you prepared, you should have a good idea about how much they will offer and what is available. You will be happier and more successful when you are a good match.

Transitions

Transitions are often a time of uncertainty; a time of adaptation and learning. You want to create a clear vision of where you want to go but need to maintain enough flexibility to take advantage of opportunities when they develop. While preparing for your transition you should pay attention to the details, especially if you are more oriented to "big picture" issues. A misspelled word in a resume can knock you out of contention for a position no matter how many positive accomplishments you list. Find someone to proof your work before you send it out. Create a system to follow through on important tasks. It will not do you much good to get networking leads if you don't call them or forget to send information you promised to them. Often it is a thank-you letter to a contact or interviewer that can make the difference between you and another candidate.

Change is a Fact of Life

No matter how much you desire stability and continuity, things change. Personal, educational and work-related organizations and belief systems prepare people for continuity, not for change. Predictability and stability are prized, and even in the face of evidence to the contrary, people often assume it that most relationships are permanent.

Planning and Action Replace Uncertainty

Planning for any transition in one's life will help facilitate a positive change. But even if one chooses not to plan, hoping that things will remain exactly as they are, they won't. Changes, even dramatic ones, will occur. Planning for change will help gain a measure of control that one would not have otherwise.

Each time you move from one stage of your life to another, you leave behind significant relationships, and you build new ones. It is normal to experience a period of uncertainty as you move into a new situation even if the situation you are leaving is unproductive or negative.

The simple acceptance of such transitions as reality, and the openness to the possibilities of the new situation, will enable you to deal positively with change and to feel more in control of your life.

Some exercises in this book will help you assess both your attitudes and expectations regarding change. One of the biggest changes anyone faces in life is seeking a new career/job. In the next exercise, you will identify realities you must consider in preparing for a life change including how past occurrences color your present attitudes, and how to gain control of any new change.

By studying changes that have you successfully managed in the past, you will realize the strengths that will enable you to manage future change confidently.

Take the positives from past

+ Let go of the negatives

+ Create clear goals =

New Opportunities

What are some of the things that concern you about change?

Significant Life Factors and Change

Throughout our lives we all experience many changes. On the next page, list changes you have been through; consider both planned and unplanned, positive and negative.

After you have reflected on changes in your life, consider how you came to select your job or career path. Too often, our ideas of what is possible are confined to what we've read, what other people we know have done, what other people expect from us, and so on.

Factors that influence our career choices include:

- Parents' education
- Parents' life and career experiences
- What did they do for a living?
- Was there a sense of continuity or disruption?
- Did your parents separation or divorce? And why?
- Ethnic and cultural background
- Parents' expectations
- Our birth orders
- Our education
- Our friends and acquaintances
- Religious beliefs
- The economy
- Where we live
- Our health
- Our skills
- Our marital status
- If we have children

List the factors that have had an influence on your career choices

Reactions to Change

Changing jobs or beginning a new career will cause you to make many adjustments in your life. The more aware you are of your behavior, the more likely that you will feel in control. As you reflect on the challenges and changes in your life, think about what you thought, felt and did. What did you learn from your experiences? What would you like to change? On the next two pages there are opportunities to list these changes. Repeat this format for other major changes.

What was the change or challenge?	
What I thought about it.	
How I felt about it.	
What I did about it.	
What I learned from it.	
What I would like to change.	

What was the change or challenge?	
What I thought about it.	
How I felt about it.	
What I did about it.	
What I learned from it.	
What I would like to change.	

What was the change or challenge?	
What I thought about it.	
How I felt about it.	
What I did about it.	
What I learned from it.	
What I would like to change.	

What was the change or challenge?	
What I thought about it.	
How I felt about it.	
What I did about it.	
What I learned from it.	
What I would like to change.	

...then I painted the garage

Ideally, you can plan your transition over time—but it doesn't always work out that way. When I was doing outplacement on a full-time basis most of my clients had relatively little choice in staying with their employer. Some people saw *the writing on the wall*; it surprised others, and they were shocked to find out they were no longer employed. Often spouses stated that they were more aware of the risk of layoff than were the employees themselves.

When people go through the loss of a job, they often go through a grieving process such as Elizabeth Kubler-Ross described in her books on death and dying. Early reactions often include shock and denial. Most people get over these feelings rather quickly, especially when they are honest about how the job they are leaving did not meet many of their needs. But there are individuals who take a while to move past the loss and focus on the future (and literally or figuratively paint the garage).

There can be lifelong desires of an around-the-world trip or continuing your education that you can pursue now a job isn't tying you down. If you are moving towards an important goal, then not going to a job may be a great opportunity. A physicist I knew went to Nepal for half a year, came back to the United States, went for an M.B.A. and changed his career.

Another positive change can occur with the opportunity of refocusing life goals. There may never be a better time to change your relationship with family and friends. Spending more time with your children while you are between jobs may alter your definition of how much time you want to spend at work. It is important to recognize the difference of moving towards a goal versus avoiding the activities of a job search.

There are also those individuals who spend an inordinate amount of time preparing for their search by creating novel tracking systems for their job search activities. One person told me he had spent two weeks working on this effort. Based on his salary, this cost him several thousand dollars compared to using available software. If you are excited by your tracking system, you are spending time better served in networking or other proactive activities.

Other behaviors to avoid include using job search methods that are relatively passive, such as sending out letters to several hundred people and then waiting to hear from them. Or finding you can't seem to get your resume perfect—so you don't send it to anyone.

For people who use a facility to work out of, such as in outplacement or within an employment services office there is a danger of "hiding out".

While it's convenient to have secretarial support and a trained career coach, it is important to not "hang out" at the office. Once you have honed your job search skills and networked with your colleagues, it is time to make other people. Too many people hide in their cubicles, complaining about how their search isn't going well. In the worst-case scenario, this behavior can lead to frustration, anger or depression.

Possibilities and Choices

You need to be open-minded and creative to explore fully all the options open to you and right for you. Here is a puzzle that illustrates this point. Will you allow yourself to find the creative solution or will you keep yourself confined to limited ways of seeing things?

Instructions: Connect all nine dots, using only 4 straight lines, without lifting your pen or pencil from the paper.

A hint: You can only solve this problem if you "think outside the box".

How Our Beliefs Affect Our Behavior

Our interpretation of actions and events, coupled with how we define ourselves, determines how we feel. Where some people see interesting challenges, others see problems. Some people will use up their energy complaining about what went wrong; some people will become energized to come up with creative solutions. We all have considerable control over how we see things—either focusing on the positive or the negative. Are you a person who sees challenges or sees problems? The point of view you choose will seriously influence your job search. This process should be repeated for each of your beliefs.

I believe that:	
I see this as a challenge because:	
I see this as a problem because:	

I believe that:	
I see this as a challenge because:	
I see this as a problem because:	

I believe that:	
I see this as a challenge because:	
I see this as a problem because:	

I believe that:	
I see this as a challenge because:	
I see this as a problem because:	

Who's in Charge Here? (Locues of Control)

One of the first steps in managing any area of your life is taking responsibility for situations you can influence. Carl Rogers refers to this as " owning " your behavior, actions, feelings and attitudes. Only then can you change them. In developing job search skills, the same principle applies. You must take responsibility for learning what you need to know. Look within yourself before looking at external factors. Being accountable to oneself rather than blaming others is a key element in achieving self-fulfillment.

Locus of control is a personality construct reflecting one's belief or perception about who controls behavior and life events. The perception identifies the place (locus) of control for what happens in life and leads to an expectancy of one's ability to control life events. The belief can exist in varying degrees, reflecting the degree to which one perceives personal control in life. The key links are between behavior and its consequences, and between outcomes and personal effort.

The range of beliefs extends from an internal to an external locus of control. The person with an internal locus believes that positive or negative events are consequences of their own actions. What a person does or doesn't do makes a difference. When a person has an external locus, their expectancy is that events are independent of their actions and not within their control.

They see little cause and effect between their behavior and its outcome. They see outside influences such as luck, chance, fate, and powerful others or societal influences controlling their lives.

It is important to reinforce that it is the individual who is the most important person in determining his or her own choices and actions. Without denying that people and events may influence the options a person has, it is the individual who has ultimate responsibility for the road he or she takes. Perhaps the most important attitude / belief that people can have in making a good adjustment to any change is that they can always choose to make the best of a situation; they can always set and work towards goals that they want to pursue.

As you do the exercises in this book, always keep in mind that the more positive you are about attaining your goals, the more likely you will succeed.

Be Aware of the Buts

As you take more charge of your decision-making and job search, know that old habits can get in your way. One of these is the word "but." Invariably, when you or someone else uses the word "but" it signifies an objection—some reason not to act. You do not have to be a victim of this kind of thinking.

Tom was a 74-year-old, draftsman, laid off from his job when the company he worked for was sold and they moved his job out of state. His coworkers thought he would retire because he was eligible for a pension and Social Security. When he informed them he intended to find a new job their response was, "Tom, you are great at what you do, but you are 74 years old.". Tom's attitude was that his age was not a problem for him and that the more he could focus on what he offered the better off he would be. I'm not saying that everyone will have the same success that Tom had (he found a job within a week); I am saying a positive attitude will help you get past other objections. Tom's successful approach to his new employer focused on his experience and how quickly he could develop plans for simple projects—hiring him was effective. He communicated a high level of enthusiasm and energy, something people much younger rarely did.

In contrast, Greg was a middle management finance professional referred after he had been unemployed for over 18 months. Frustrated and angry, he had gone through his savings and was feeling desperate. When I asked him why he thought he had not found a job yet he had dozens of reasons; none were his responsibility. He said he had followed every bit of advice offered "but none of it has worked". He used the "but" to protect himself. Greg's problem was not what he was doing in his job search; it was how he did it. He was so frustrated that his attitude had become pugnacious—his anger came across to the people he needed to talk to. Eventually, using a tape recorder and a mirror, Greg could see and hear how he presented himself. With some practice (he had to smile in the mirror before he could make a phone call) he found a new, satisfactory position. It was getting awareness of his behavior and taking control that solved his problem.

Reframing

Once you take responsibility for your career choices and are willing to "think outside the box" it is important to develop a skill called reframing.

Reframing refers to changing the way you and others perceive things. Is the glass half full or half empty; are you faced with a problem or a challenge? During your career assessment and job search it is important that you can be flexible in how you define things to yourself and communicate them to others.

Denise worked as a lobbyist for an association where she made and maintained contacts with a wide variety of people, both within and outside of the organization. She needed to be outgoing, friendly and persuasive. When the position ended she convinced the head of a large career counseling organization she had the skills to both sell and deliver the company's services. How different was it to convince legislators to buy into the issues she was selling compared to selling services to different organizations and companies? In addition, she was a natural counselor, having developed empathy, and gained the ability to communicate effectively. By thinking "outside the box" (see page 21) she could transition into a new career using the same core strengths that had made her successful in the past. The secret is to convincingly redefine yourself. To do that, you must understand your core strengths.

Lou, a job candidate, was questioned about his sales experience (of which he had little) and how he would handle the stress of having to sell as part of the job. Rather than state he did not have the experience that the employer was looking for or answer evasively, Lou answered by first asking a question—did the employer agree that he had a responsible position where (1) he had been persuasive and (2) there was a high level of stress? The employer acknowledged that this was the case. Lou then described parallels between his experiences and that of successful salespeople. This included using accomplishments that highlighted persuasion, assertiveness, empathy and resilience. He got the job offer.

Gretchen had been a Director of Nursing and Manager of Quality for a major hospital chain. She wanted variety, lots of contact with people, and new challenges. When she lost her job through a downsizing, she thought she would have to look for a job she had already done, Director of Nursing, or a lower level job because of her age (mid 50's). We looked at her skills and energy level and went in a new direction. Within a month she had a new position with a major corporation. She would help introduce new technology to nurses and she would do it for more money than her last job had paid.

Doris had been an accounts receivable clerk for a company that produced specialty chemicals. When the company moved, she did not move with them, and she would not have been comfortable in doing so. Her initial reaction was despair. Where would she find a job? Another specialty chemical company had just closed a mile from where she worked, and Doris felt that there were few choices available to her. She had defined herself so narrowly that she was sure she would be unemployed for a long time. Through a thorough assessment process Doris realized that her skills were broader than she had realized and that her interests included being helpful to the elderly, for instance, helping her own mother and doing volunteer work. She reframed her skills and got a position with a nursing home as a bookkeeper. She was thrilled with her new position.

Bruce was an accomplished social worker and administrator who was looking for new challenges. He had a strong interest in computers and was constantly advancing his knowledge in this area. When an opportunity arose to contribute to his organization's need to improve its IT and billing procedures, he volunteered. Several years later he runs the IT department for a major institution.

Perfect Work Environment

Think about what you would consider an ideal work environment. Develop work goals to determine what would make that environment a reality. Write down the specifics of:

Physical environment:

The characteristics of the work tasks:

The relationships among the personnel:

The benefits that you gain from the total work environment (money, benefits, training)

Any other factors or situations that you feel are important to the creation of an ideal work environment

- 2 - Evaluate

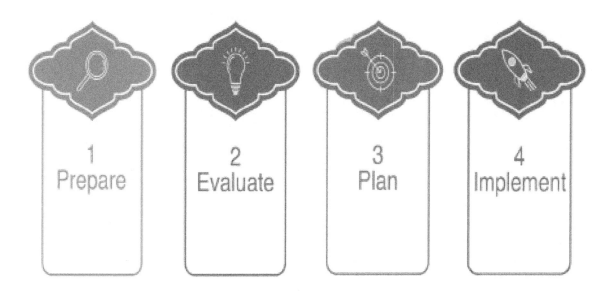

1
Prepare

2
Evaluate

3
Plan

4
Implement

What to Expect in this Section

Identifying Core Strengths

Can Do - Will Do - Fit

When you combine your abilities with the motivation to follow through, you have determined your strengths. You should try to find a match between your strengths and the requirements of a job. There are three key issues when an employer considers you for a job.

The first factor is can you do the job?

This includes such factors as having sufficient skills and training, meeting educational requirements, getting the required certificate or license, and being physically capable of doing the job.

The second factor is will you do the job?

Are you motivated? Do you understand what is expected? This goes beyond having a set of skills regarding baking, business knowledge, automobile repair, or secretarial duties. It includes having the right attitudes toward working and getting along with other people, communicating effectively, developing maturity, and making a commitment.

The third factor is how well will you fit with a specific work environment?

We all have a set of preferences and tendencies regarding what kind of environment will help us be the happiest and most productive. Each work place has a style and culture that has developed over time. It is important to understand how the individual and the environment work together, and how to create a match that will maximize the likelihood of a productive, satisfying fit (examples: some people are extroverted, others introverted; some people prefer a lot of structure, other do well in a more flexible workplace). Employers need to be clear about their expectations for performance in each of the above areas.

So, do you.

What does it take to be successful in their organization? As a candidate for a position it is important for you to take responsibility to match the needs of the organization with your own strengths and goals.

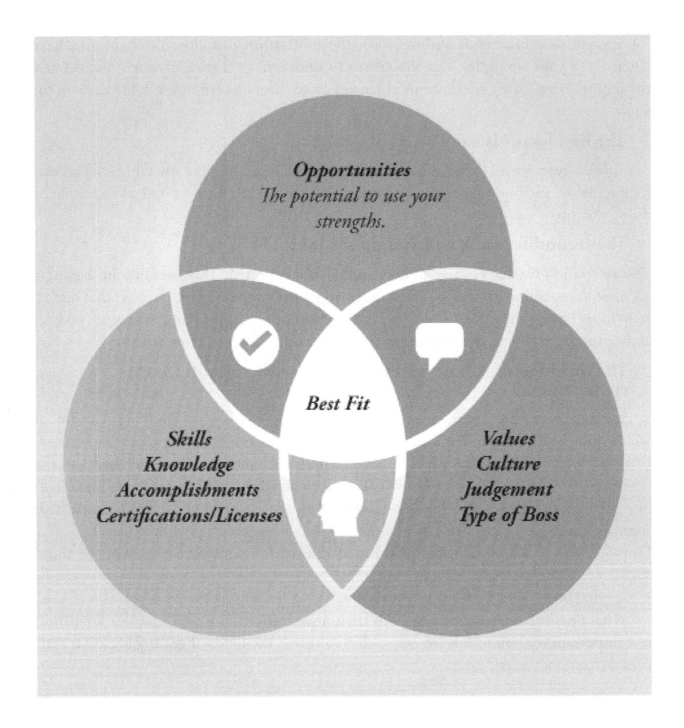

Reviewing Accomplishments

An important step in your career development is the identification of accomplishments and strengths.

Awareness of your accomplishments:

Being aware of your accomplishments helps you:

- Improves your ability to communicate your value to an organization (for example, an accomplishment can be used to tell a story about what you have done in the past and could do for someone else. Selected accomplishments should also be included in your resume.)

- Improves your confidence and self-esteem.

- Helps you identify generic skills and strengths that could be used in new ways.

Accomplishments are actions that have given you satisfaction and a sense of pride. They demonstrate your productivity, which results from your efforts, whether operating alone or with others, which improve a situation. Abilities are contained in, and reflected by, accomplishments.

The purpose of reviewing accomplishments is to focus your energies on what you well; to reinforce your abilities, and to communicate your achievements, competencies, knowledge, and strengths.

An accomplishment can be large or small in scope, routine or extraordinary, frequent or something you have done only once, work related or personal. Take the time to learn about and be able to express your accomplishments.

On the following pages are a list of action verbs.

- Review them before you complete the accomplishment work sheets that follow.

- Use the list of verbs to trigger your thinking about the things you have accomplished.

- Use these verbs in place of vague, general verbs like "worked on," "joined," or "did."

- Note how much more effective the sentence "I edited the employee handbook" is than "I worked on the employee handbook."

Action Verbs

Achieved	Acquired	Acted	Activated
Adapted	Addressed	Administered	Adopted
Advised	Analyzed	Appointed	Appraised
Approved	Arbitrated	Arranged	Ascertained
Assembled	Assessed	Assisted	Attained
Audited	Averted	Advertised	Balanced
Budgeted	Built	Calculated	Centralized
Charted	Checked	Classified	Coached
Collaborated	Collected	Combined	Communicated
Compiled	Completed	Composed	Computed
Conceived	Conceptualized	Condensed	Conducted
Conferred	Connected	Conserved	Consolidated
Constructed	Consulted	Controlled	Converted
Coordinated	Corrected	Correlated	Counseled
Created	Decided	Decreased	Defined
Delivered	Demonstrated	Designed	Detailed
Detected	Determined	Developed	Devised
Diagnosed	Directed	Discovered	Dispensed
Displayed	Distributed	Diverted	Documented
Doubled	Drafted	Dramatized	Drew
Edited	Educated	Elected	Eliminated
Employed	Enforced	Engineered	Enlisted

Ensured	Established	Estimated	Evaluated
Examined	Expanded	Expedited	Experimented
Explained	Extended	Extracted	Facilitated
Finalized	Financed	Fired	Forecast
Formed	Fostered	Found	Founded
Furnished	Generated	Governed	Guaranteed
Guided	Handled	Headed	Helped
Hired	Hypothesized	Identified	Illustrated
Implemented	Improvised	Increased	Influenced
Informed	Initiated	Innovated	Inspected
Installed	Instituted	Integrated	Interpreted
Interviewed	Introduced	Invented	Invested
Investigated	Judged	Launched	Lectured
Led	Liquidated	Logged	Made
Maintained	Managed	Manipulated	Mapped
Marketed	Matched	Mediated	Met
Modeled	Modernized	Modified	Monitored
Motivated	Navigated	Negotiated	Nominated
Observed	Obtained	Offered	Opened
Operated	Orchestrated	Organized	Originated
Oversaw	Parted	Participated	Perceived
Performed	Photographed	Piloted	Pioneered
Planned	Predicted	Prepared	Prescribed

Presented	Prevented	Processed	Procured
Produced	Programmed	Projected	Promoted
Proposed	Protected	Proved	Publicized
Published	Purchased	Raised	Read
Realized	Recommended	Reasoned	Received
Reconciled	Reconstructed	Recorded	Recruited
Redesigned	Reduced	Referred	Refined
Rehabilitated	Reinforced	Related	Rendered
Reorganized	Reported	Represented	Researched
Resolved	Responded	Restored	Restructured
Retrieved	Reviewed	Revised	Revitalized
Resolved	Responded	Restored	Restructured
Retrieved	Reviewed	Revised	Revitalized
Salvaged	Satisfied	Scheduled	Secured
Selected	Separated	Served	Shaped
Shared	Showed	Simplified	Sketched
Sold	Solved	Spearheaded	Staffed
Spearheaded	Staffed	Standardized	Streamlined
Structured	Studied	Submitted	Summarized
Supervised	Supplemented	Supplied	Surveyed
Scheduled	Secured	Selected	Separated
Served	Shaped	Shared	Showed
Simplified	Sketched	Sold	Solved
Spearheaded	Staffed	Standardized	Streamlined

Structured	Studied	Submitted	Summarized
Supervised	Supplemented	Supplied	Surveyed
Symbolized	Synergized	Synthesized	Systematized
Tabulated	Tailored	Taught	Tended
Tested	Trained	Transacted	Transcribed
Translated	Traveled	Treated	Tutored
Uncovered	Wrote		

Accomplishment Work Sheets

For each accomplishment, describe the:

Challenge, situation or problem.

- Tell what you needed to do and the difficulties you confronted.

Actions you took to improve the situation.

- These should show your knowledge and good judgment. Your actions could include you working as part of a team.

Results.

- Quantify them when possible. It is easier for people to remember specific, objective results than vague generalities, so a quantified description of your accomplishments has a more positive impact.

Do this with a minimum of six accomplishments. At least four should be from your work experience. The more experience you have the more achievements you should be able to list. If you have worked for 10 years and have done only two valuable things per year, you should be able to generate 20 accomplishments. If your work gets organized by projects, each completed project should produce at least one accomplishment.

Most people seem to take for granted those skills they use regularly. Unless you share this information with others, they may never realize your talents. For example, customer service skills are an important part of many (most?) jobs but often overlooked by the people who see it as an ingrained part of their position.

This is not the time for false modesty. We are not talking about bragging; just be clear about real contributions you have made.

One source of accomplishments is past performance appraisals. List assignments you have worked on and the outcome of your efforts. An engineer I worked with was leaving a large petrochemical firm after 30 years. The company had kept track of his accomplishments; he had a list of 138.

Make copies of the accomplishments work sheet as you continue to develop your list.

Accomplishment 1:

Describe the challenge, situation, or problem:

What action did you take to improve the situation:

What resulted from your action?

Accomplishment 2:

Describe the challenge, situation, or problem:

What action did you take to improve the situation:

What resulted from your action?

Accomplishment 3:

Describe the challenge, situation, or problem:

What action did you take to improve the situation:

What resulted from your action?

Accomplishment 4:

Describe the challenge, situation, or problem:

What action did you take to improve the situation:

What resulted from your action?

Accomplishment 5:

Describe the challenge, situation, or problem:

What action did you take to improve the situation:

What resulted from your action?

Accomplishment 6:

Describe the challenge, situation, or problem:

What action did you take to improve the situation:

What resulted from your action?

Transferable Skills List

Review this list of transferable skills. Place an X next to all you have used. This includes skills from your business experience, home life, hobbies and volunteer activities. Then, go back and put a second X next to those activities you would enjoy doing again.

Used this Skill	Would do Again	Transferable Skill	Used this Skill	Would do Again	Transferable Skill
		Adapt To Situations			Confront Others
		Advise People			Construct Buildings
		Analyze Data			Contact Others
		Anticipate Problems			Contract With Others
		Appraise Service			Control Costs
		Arrange Functions			Control People
		Assemble Equipment			Control Situations
		Assess Situations			Cooperate With Others
		Audit Records			Coordinate Activities
		Bargain/Barter			Cope With Deadlines
		Budget Money			Copy Information
		Build			Cost Conscious
		Buy Products/Services			Create
		Calculate Numbers			Delegate
		Chart Information			Deliver

Used this Skill	Would do Again	Transferable Skill	Used this Skill	Would do Again	Transferable Skill
		Check For Accuracy			Demonstrate
		Classify Information			Design
		Come Up With Ideas			Detail
		Communicate With Others			Detect
		Compare Data			Determine
		Compile Statistics			Develop
		Compute Data			Direct Others
		Conduct			Distribute
		Draft			Handle Money
		Drive			Help People
		Edit			Imagine Solutions
		Encourage			Implement
		Entertain			Improve
		Establish			Improvise
		Estimate			Inform People
		Evaluate			Initiate Actions
		Examine			Inspect Products
		Exchange			Instruct

Used this Skill	Would do Again	Transferable Skill	Used this Skill	Would do Again	Transferable Skill
		Exhibit			Interpret Data
		Expand			Interview People
		Expedite			Invent
		Explain			Inventory
		Explore			Investigate
		File Records			Lead People
		Find Information			Learn
		Fix / Repair			Liaison
		Follow Directions			Lift (Heavy)
		Follow Through			Lift (Moderate)
		Gather Information			Listen
		Gather Materials			Locate Information
		Generate			Log Information
		Guide / Lead			Logic
		Hand / Eye Coordination			Maintenance
		Handle Complaints			Make / Create
		Handle Equipment			Make Decisions
		Handle Materials			Manage A Business

Used this Skill	Would do Again	Transferable Skill	Used this Skill	Would do Again	Transferable Skill
		Manage People			Print
		Measure Boundaries			Process Information
		Mediate Problems			Process Materials
		Meet The Public			Productions
		Memorize Information			Program
		Mentor Others			Promote
		Monitor Progress			Public Relations
		Motivate Others			Question Others
		Move Materials			Quickly Learn
		Negotiate			Quickly Work
		Nurse			Raise Money
		Nurture			Read Reference Books
		Observe			Recommend
		Operate Equipment			Record Data
		Order Goods/ Supplies			Recruit People
		Organize Data			Rectify
		Organize Equipment			Reduce Costs
		Organize People			Refer People

Used this Skill	Would do Again	Transferable Skill	Used this Skill	Would do Again	Transferable Skill
		Own / Operate Business			Rehabilitate People
		Paint			Remember Information
		Perceive Needs			Remove
		Perform Routine Work			Repair
		Persuade Others			Replace
		Plan			Report Information
		Plant			Research
		Policy Making			Resolve Problems
		Precision Work			Responsible For
		Prepare Materials			Restore
		Retrieve Information			Study
		Review			Supply
		Run Meetings			Survey
		Schedule			Synthesize
		Seek Out			Tabulate
		Select			Take Action/Perform
		Sell			Take Instructions
		Separate			Tend Equipment

Used this Skill	Would do Again	Transferable Skill	Used this Skill	Would do Again	Transferable Skill
		Sequence			Test
		Service Customers			Think Ahead
		Service Equipment			Tolerate Interruptions
		Set Goals / Objectives			Train / Teach
		Set Up Equipment			Transcribe
		Set Up Systems			Translate
		Sew			Treat
		Shape			Type
		Size Up Situations			Update Info
		Socialize			Visualize
		Solve Problems			Write Procedures
		Sort			Write Reports
		Speak In Public			

Marketable Assets

You are a valued product.

One way to explore your career possibilities is to consider yourself as a product that has perceived value by potential employers. What are people looking for and how can you package yourself in such a way you will be attractive? All the employers I interviewed saw certain characteristics as important. These included having a good attitude and being flexible. The workplace is changing so rapidly that employers appreciate people who will make adjustments to meet the needs of the organization.

Marketing professionals talk about features and benefits of a product. Features are characteristics of the product, such as a car may have four doors and anti-lock brakes. Benefits might include ease of use or safety because of those features.

Depending on the position you are seeking, the following characteristics can be features and/or benefits. Consider which of these characteristics you have and how perspective employers may view them:

Managerial experience	Strong industry background
Good interpersonal skills	Meets deadlines
Startup experience	Turnaround success
New account development	Superior client relationships
Meets goals	Budget responsibility
Sales experience	New product introduction
Increase in market share	Analytical abilities
Contract negotiation	National account management
Computer skills	High energy level
Language ability	Advanced degree/education
Flexible	Training experience
Strategic planning	Recruiting/hiring

Downsizing experience	International experience
Public speaking	Written communication
Bottom line responsibility	Motivator
Various equipment experiences	Administrative skills
Clerical skills	Self starter/shows initiative
Financial expertise	Loyalty
Human resources expertise	Works well with people
Add additional assets below	Add additional assets below

Defining Strengths from Accomplishments

Look at each of your accomplishments and consider what skills, behavioral preferences and motivation went into the strengths you used to make the accomplishment happen. Use the checklists you completed on skills for appropriate words. This will help you explain to someone else what your strengths are. Use the space below to define strengths for each accomplishment.

Accomplishment 1
Accomplishment 2
Accomplishment 3

Accomplishment 4

Accomplishment 5

Accomplishment 6

Accomplishment 7

Good Judgement

When employers consider you for a job, they evaluate you to see if you have good judgment. While some decisions are definitely connected to your values and motivation, other choices are related to making the right decision at the right time. This is what Daniel Goleman refers to as *Emotional Intelligence*. As much as knowledge is important to completing an assignment, so is the ability to choose wisely.

Consider situations where you have demonstrated good judgment and give examples. These situations will show how you and others around you benefit from the choices you have made regarding working with others and handling various tasks. These may or may not overlap with your accomplishments. Think of decisions you have made at work that have had a good outcome. One example would be that you have made good hiring decisions.

Decisions I made at work that resulted in good outcomes:

Self-Assessment of Personal Attributes

The forms on the following pages can help you identify how you see yourself in the world of work in terms of job-related personality factors. It uses definitions from *Caliper Corporation*.

With this information, you can compare your perception of yourself with other managers and professionals and consider the personal attributes required in various jobs and careers.

What the Profile Does:

With a better sense of your job-related personal attributes, you will be in a stronger position to create a successful career development plan.

The profile lists attributes used to describe the ways people behave, think, and feel in different positions in different work settings on the following page.

This exercise is your personal evaluation of your job-related personality factors.

Toward the end of this manual I provide another form to get feedback from others regarding these same behavior.

For an in-depth analysis, taking the full Caliper profile from our organization can provide invaluable data.

Directions:

Read through each statement.

To the right of each of the attributes, you will find a 10-point scale for rating how you see yourself. Below each of the attribute headings are phrases that describe someone who rates himself/herself high on the scale. Consider past and present career activities as a context and consider each attribute. Use other managers and professionals as a context for rating and comparing yourself.

How do you rank yourself?

Circle the one number on the scale which best reflects your sense of how you compare to other managers and professionals on the attribute.

When you have finished the survey:

You will have the opportunity to rank the attributes you see as your strengths.

1= Lowest; 10=Highest
Persuasive 1 2 3 4 5 6 7 8 9 10
The innate need to persuade others as a means of gaining personal satisfaction. Individuals scoring high on persuasion will tend to seek other people's commitment for the sheer satisfaction of winning through persuasion
Assertiveness 1 2 3 4 5 6 7 8 9 10
Assertiveness is the ability to express one's thoughts forcefully and consistently without having to rely on anger. Those with a low score on this characteristic are not comfortable communicating their ideas and opinions in a direct manner and tend to be more reluctant to confront issues.
Aggressiveness 1 2 3 4 5 6 7 8 9 10
This is an emotion-based way of expressing oneself and tends to be more reactive than proactive. Unlike assertiveness, individuals who have high aggressiveness may be "heavy-handed" in their approach in "getting their way". Some degree of aggressiveness can be valuable. Those with a low score may be uncomfortable when it comes to supporting a position where there is-resistance
Resilience 1 2 3 4 5 6 7 8 9 10
Resilience is the ability to handle rejection and accept criticism in a manner that is constructive and growth oriented. People high in resilience tend to have a healthy, intact ego and a positive self-image. Those scoring low tend to be more self-critical and less tolerant of critical feedback and rejection.
Urgency 1 2 3 4 5 6 7 8 9 10
Urgency is an inner-directed and focused need to get things done. Extremely high scores indicate impatience or unrealistic expectations. Low levels indicate patience or a potential for complacency.
Risk Taking 1 2 3 4 5 6 7 8 9 10
This quality reflects the degree of comfort one has taking chances or trying new things. It does not imply recklessness (i.e.; one can be a calculated risk taker). People scoring high in this area may be intrigued by taking chances and trying new things. Those with a low score tend to prefer conventional or well-established methods.
Empathy 1 2 3 4 5 6 7 8 9 10
Empathy is the ability to accurately sense the reactions of another person. People with high levels of empathy can "put themselves in the other person's shoes" (not necessarily agree with the other person).
Cautiousness 1 2 3 4 5 6 7 8 9 10
This characteristic relates to the speed with which one is comfortable in making decisions. Very high rankings indicate the need to make decisions slowly.

1= Lowest; 10=Highest
Sociability 1 2 3 4 5 6 7 8 9 10
Sociability is defined as a need to seek out the company and camaraderie of others. Such individuals relate well in one-on-one situations. People who rank low are usually more comfortable when they are not expected to interface on a regular basis with a wide variety of people.
Gregariousness 1 2 3 4 5 6 7 8 9 10
Gregariousness is extroverted, ebullient optimism. Gregarious people are outgoing and enjoy working with large groups; they have a genuine enjoyment of social interaction. Those scoring low in this area can be reserved and uncomfortable in new, unknown social situations.
Accommodation 1 2 3 4 5 6 7 8 9 10
Individuals who have high scores in this dimension tends to be helpful and service oriented. They also have a need to be liked, respond to recognition, and work hard to please others. Those scoring low do not feel a strong need to get approval.
Skepticism 1 2 3 4 5 6 7 8 9 10
Skepticism is a doubting or questioning state of mind. Individuals scoring high in this quality tend to be suspicious of others' motivations. Low levels on this scale suggest possible naiveté.
Self-Structure 1 2 3 4 5 6 7 8 9 10
Self-structure indicates a preference for determining one's own priorities and methods for managing tasks. People with high scores tend to be self-disciplined. They are able to coordinate multiple activities and typically are good at organizing activities. People with low scores may require help and direction when defining and setting priorities. They may be more comfortable in an environment where parameters and guidelines are established and communicated.
External-Structure 1 2 3 4 5 6 7 8 9 10
Individuals scoring high in external structure are sensitive to externally-defined rules, policies and procedures. They operate with some sensitivity to authority and will generally prefer a working environment in which direction is set.
Energy 1 2 3 4 5 6 7 8 9 10
This is in reference to psychological energy. Individuals with high-energy scores tend to want to do many things on a given day, are able to move from task to task without tiring, and are quite willing to do hard work. There are several possible reasons for a low energy score including personal distractions.
Openness 1 2 3 4 5 6 7 8 9 10
People high in openness are open-minded and perceive different points of view. Individuals low in openness avoid ideas different from those they already hold.

Job Related Strengths

List in rank order of importance the 7 attributes you see as your strengths.
How does this list compare to your other strength list?

#1
#2
#3
#4
#5
#6
#7

20 Qualities to Describe You

This is a fun and enlightening exercise to begin the self-discovery process. I have found that it has been used in management and career development, and as an acting exercise. Go to 20 people and ask them to describe you in just one word, write them below in the line marked *Quality*. After each word write down two examples of how you have demonstrated that quality.

- Are there any surprises?
- Is this how you would describe yourself to others?

Quality 1:
I have demonstrated this quality by:
1.
2.
Quality 2:
I have demonstrated this quality by:
1.
2.
Quality 3:
I have demonstrated this quality by:
1.
2.
Quality 4:
I have demonstrated this quality by:
1.
2.
Quality 5:
I have demonstrated this quality by:
1.
2.

Quality 6:
I have demonstrated this quality by:
1.
2.
Quality 7:
I have demonstrated this quality by:
1.
2.
Quality 8:
I have demonstrated this quality by:
1.
2.
Quality 9:
I have demonstrated this quality by:
1.
2.
Quality 10:
I have demonstrated this quality by:
1.
2.
Quality 11:
I have demonstrated this quality by:
1.
2.
Quality 12:
I have demonstrated this quality by:
1.
2.

Quality 13:

I have demonstrated this quality by:

1.

2.

Quality 14:

I have demonstrated this quality by:

1.

2.

Quality 15:

I have demonstrated this quality by:

1.

2.

Quality 16:

I have demonstrated this quality by:

1.

2.

Quality 17:

I have demonstrated this quality by:

1.

2.

Quality 18;

I have demonstrated this quality by:

1.

2.

Quality 19;

I have demonstrated this quality by:

1.

2.

Quality 20;

I have demonstrated this quality by:

1.

2.

Values

What we value can have a great influence on determining what makes up the right employment. What seems like an ideal environment for one person can be awful for another. And, what you consider important at one time in your life may change, affecting the choices you make.

> *Bill was an Assistant Comptroller who, during our preliminary discussions, stated that his previous employment had taken up too much of his time. He had worked long hours plus had a considerable commute. He had two young children and felt he did not spend enough time with them. During his job search he developed two job offers and had to decide which one to accept. One paid considerably more than the other but would also increase his commute by at least an hour every day. He took the job that would allow him to attend his son's Little League games and his daughter's dance classes. As he told me, "I only have one opportunity to see them grow up".*

> *Anita was an expert in Pacific Rim Economics in her early thirties. She conducted a very effective job search and had multiple offers. She made her choice based on where she felt she could have the best mentor. She could have started at a higher salary in another position but felt the long- term career potential would be greater with the support from her coach.*

> *John had been a manager for a Fortune 50 corporation. He was divorced and his children were grown. He wanted greater autonomy and a healthier environment. When we targeted organization he might like to work for we focused on smaller companies where there was greater opportunity to take on more responsibility. He was open to moving, especially if it was to somewhere where the weather was warmer. He took a position with a small, start-up who valued his marketing expertise and became president of the firm.*

Charlie was a Comptroller who lost his position following a restructuring. When we discussed his background and interests, I discovered that he had a strong interest in jazz. We decided that he would check out jobs where he could combine his love of music with his marketable talents. He developed an opportunity at a radio station that featured jazz.

Sheila had a successful career at a large company but decided that there was too much stress in her life. She and her life partner researched places they would like to live and explored how they would support themselves. They bought property in a small town out west and started their own business.

Sara got a good paying job at a company that produced a tobacco product. She passed on the position because she felt that tobacco caused health problems, and she did not want to contribute anything that might promote the product.

Al was the executive of a well-known company. He had a very successful career and was up for a promotion that would require him to move to another state. After discussing the move with his wife and children he decided that moving would disrupt his family. They had strong ties to the community, friends, and family. He decided that he should pass on the promotion and look for something that would allow him to remain in his home state. Al became the President of a major corporation—in his home state.

Select the Values that Are Most Important to You

Values are preferences regarding appropriate actions or outcomes. Values reflect a person's sense of right or wrong or what ought to be. Values reflect what you think is important in life.

Please put a check mark next to the values important to you.

	Comfort		Sincerity
	Learning environment		Health
	Honesty		Physical activity
	Caring		Creativity
	Teaching		Working conditions
	Health		Artistic expression
	Standard of living		Intimacy
	Dynamic environment		Kindness
	Recreation		Integrity
	Money		Helpfulness
	Teamwork		Status
	Accomplishment		Nature
	Recognition		Autonomy
	Time with family		Power
	Freedom		Opportunities for advancement
	Belonging		Equality
	Security		Travel
	Clothes		Spirituality
	Innovation		Low stress
	Friendship		

List 7 of the values you have checked intheir approximate order of importance.

Value 1
Value 2
Value 3
Value 4
Value 5
Value 6
Value 7

Maslow's Hierarchy of Human Needs

In most cases, people prioritize their desires based on a hierarchy of needs. You are most likely to focus on basic survival issues before you are concerned about getting the right title or a corner office (there are those individuals who are the exception. You know who you are).

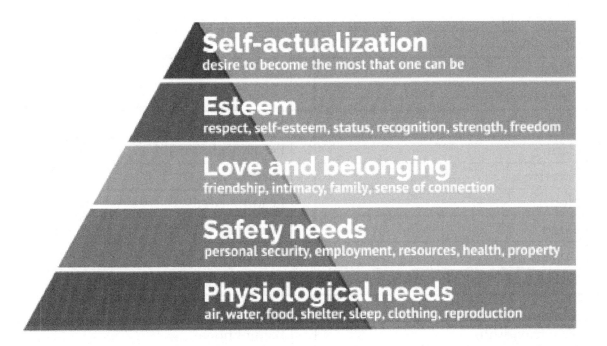

Abraham Maslow developed a model of how he saw people setting goals for themselves. People focus on the higher-level concerns after they meet basic needs. How do you prioritize your goals?

- Self-actualization needs: need for self-fulfillment and realizing one's own individual potentialities
- Esteem needs: need for achievement, approval, competence, recognition
- Love needs: need for affiliation, acceptance and belonging
- Safety needs: need to feel secure and safe, out of danger
- Physiological needs hunger, thirst, air, etc.

What Motivates You?

A combination of factors motivates most people. What motivates you in your work? Check the important factors.

	Challenging		Being Helpful
	Appreciation		Analyzing
	Changing		Intimacy
	Money		Familiar
	Problem Solving		Security
	Goal fulfillment		Stability
	Caring		Prerequisites or Privileges
	Creative		Varied
	Honesty		Leading edge
	Large		Learning
	Comfortable		Innovative
	Travel		Record-setting
	To serve		Rank
	New friendships		Being known
	Dynamic		Planning
	Important		Pastoral
	Craftsmanship		International
	Autonomy		Small
	Openness		Managing
	Adventure		Novelty
	Presenting		Feeling useful
	Fun		Uncomplicated
	Friendly		Growing
	Artistry		Unusual
	Inspirational		Peaceful
	Competitive		Aggressive
	Fair		Hands-on

What six factors are most important to you (in approximate order)?

1.	
2.	
3.	
4.	
5.	
6.	

Likes and Dislikes

It is important to learn from your experiences. Think about previous work situations.
- Using the forms on the next three pages:
- List the Title of the position.
- List the dates you were employed in this position.
- List the things you liked about the position. You can include experiences in education.

When you are finished, review your answers.
- Do you see patterns?
- When you look at your dislikes, can you conceive of things that you can do to improve the situation? For instance, if you always have a poor relationship with your boss, maybe you are contributing to the problem.

| **Title of Previous Position:** |
| **Dates of Employment:** |
| **What I Liked About the Position:** |
| 1. |
| 2. |
| 3. |
| 4. |
| 5. |
| **What I Disliked About the Position:** |
| 1. |
| 2. |
| 3. |
| 4. |
| 5. |

| **Title of Previous Position:** |
| **Dates of Employment:** |
| **What I Liked About the Position:** |
| 1. |
| 2. |
| 3. |
| 4. |
| 5. |
| **What I Disliked About the Position:** |
| 1. |
| 2. |
| 3. |
| 4. |
| 5. |

Title of Previous Position:
Dates of Employment:
What I Liked About the Position:
1.
2.
3.
4.
5.
What I Disliked About the Position:
1.
2.
3.
4.
5.

Title of Previous Position:
Dates of Employment:
What I Liked About the Position:
1.
2.
3.
4.
5.
What I Disliked About the Position:
1.
2.
3.
4.
5.

| **Title of Previous Position:** |
| **Dates of Employment:** |
| **What I Liked About the Position:** |
| 1. |
| 2. |
| 3. |
| 4. |
| 5. |
| **What I Disliked About the Position:** |
| 1. |
| 2. |
| 3. |
| 4. |
| 5. |

| **Title of Previous Position:** |
| **Dates of Employment:** |
| **What I Liked About the Position:** |
| 1. |
| 2. |
| 3. |
| 4. |
| 5. |
| **What I Disliked About the Position:** |
| 1. |
| 2. |
| 3. |
| 4. |
| 5. |

Holland Occupational Types

The *Holland Occupational Types* examine the interests that people have who perform various kinds of jobs.

People with similar interests enjoy and do well in occupations that share common activities and environments. Therefore, people who enjoy various activities where they can be helpful to others are more likely to do well in occupations that include the opportunity to be of service to others. While this may seem obvious to some people, many others overlook this simple concept in making career choices.

Holland believed by choosing your three highest interests (out of the six mentioned below), you could explain your interests in every occupation. The *Strong Interest Inventory* and the *Self-Directed Search* both make use of this model and are helpful in making a career choice. They can also expand the number of occupations you might consider for yourself.

Circle three words that best describe your interests.

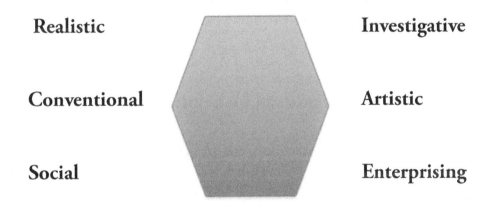

Realistic   **Investigative**

Conventional   **Artistic**

Social   **Enterprising**

Myers-Briggs Type Indicator

The *Myers-Briggs Type Indicator* (MBTI) was developed after World War II to help servicemen reenter the civilian workforce.

It matched their personalities to the behavior necessary to carry out a job. MBTI has grown in popularity and is used in the business world to gain insight into of how people's behaviors differ from each other.

A simple exercise to get you to understand behavioral tendencies is the following: Write your name. Now use the other hand. What was the difference in how it felt to you?

While you can write with either hand, one comes naturally; the other takes concentrated effort and is more difficult for you.

The same idea of behavioral preference exists for the follow categories.

When you work with your preferences your day goes more smoothly, and you feel energized rather than drained.

The instrument on the following pages is not the *Myers-Briggs Type Indicator* but has questions that deal with the same issues and should produce similar results. If you are interested, you can contact me to have the MBTI administered.

The following generalizations can be helpful in applying the Personal Preference Survey:

- Pay attention to the interviewer's personal preferences during the interview.
- Adjust your style to match theirs (as long as you are not being dishonest)
- People who have the same preferences will seem to click, to arrive at decisions more quickly, and to be on the same wavelength. They get along better. That is the positive. Ease of communication can help in the interview and in the job.
- The more differences in preference, the greater the potential for conflict and misunderstanding of each other.
- People will normally gravitate toward others who have similar preferences, although people of differing types are sometimes drawn to one another because the strengths of one are admired and needed by the other. For example, someone who hates details wants to hire someone who is good with details.
- Remember, these are preferences, sometimes mild, sometimes strong. When considering a position, how flexible will you need to be?

Personal Preference Survey

The Personal Preference Survey gives you a picture of your preferences.

Just as people have a physical preference to using their right or left hand, so they also have personality preferences: extroversion-introversion, fact oriented versus possibilities, decision making based on thinking versus feelings, preferring structure versus flexibility. Just as no person's physical preference is right or wrong, no person's personality preference is right or wrong.

Instructions: The following items are arranged in pairs (a and b) and each member of the pair represents a preference you may or may not hold. Rate your preference for each item by giving it a score of 0 to 5 (0 meaning you strongly do not prefer the statement, 5 meaning you strongly prefer the statement. The scores for a and b must add up to five (0 and 5, 1 and 4, 2 and 3, etc.) Do not use fractions.

I prefer:

	1a. making decisions after finding out what others think.
	1b. making decisions without consulting others.
	Total
	2a. being called imaginative or intuitive.
	2b. being called factual or accurate.
	Total
	3a. making decisions about people in organizations based on available data and systematic analysis of situations.
	3b. making decisions about people in organizations based on empathy feelings, and understanding their needs and wants.
	Total
	4a. allowing commitments to occur if others want to make them.
	4b. pushing for definite commitments to ensure that they are made.
	Total
	5a. quiet, thoughtful time alone.
	5b. active, energetic time with people.
	Total
	6a. using methods I know well that are effective to get the job done.
	6b. trying to think of new methods of doing tasks.
	Total

	7a. drawing conclusions based on unemotional, logical and careful step-by-step analysis.
	7b. drawing conclusions based on what I feel and believe about life.
	Total
	8a. avoid making deadlines.
	8b. setting a schedule and sticking to it.
	Total
	9a. talking awhile and then thinking to myself about a subject.
	9b. talking freely for an extended period and thinking to myself at a later time.
	Total
	10a. thinking about possibilities.
	10b. deal with actualities.
	Total
	11a. being thought of as a thinking person.
	11b. being thought of as a feeling person.
	Total
	12a. considering every possible angle for a long time before and after making a decision.
	12b. getting the information I need, considering it for a while, and making a fairly quick decision.
	Total
	13a. inner thoughts and feelings others cannot see.
	13b. activities and occurrences in which others join in.
	Total
	14a. the abstract or theoretical.
	14b. the concrete or real.
	Total
	15a. helping others explore their feelings
	15b. helping others make logical decisions.
	Total
	16a. change and keeping options open.
	16b. predictability and knowing in advance.
	Total
	17a. communicating little of my inner thinking and feelings.
	17b. communicating freely of my inner thinking and feelings.
	Total

	18a. possible views of the whole.
	18b. the factual details available.
	Total
	19a. using common sense and conviction to make decisions.
	19b. using data, analysis and reason to make decisions.
	Total
	20a. planning ahead based on projections.
	20b. planning as necessities arise, just before carrying out plans.
	Total
	21a. meeting new people
	21b. being alone or with one person I know well.
	Total
	22a. ideas.
	22b. facts.
	Total
	23a. convictions.
	23b. verifiable facts.
	Total
	24a. keeping care track of appointments and notes about commitments
	24b. using appointment books and notes as minimally as possible.
	Total
	25a. discussing a new, unconsidered issue at length in a group.
	25b. puzzling out issues in my head before sharing results with other people.
	Total
	26a. carrying out carefully laid out plans with precision.
	26b. designing plans and structures without necessarily carrying them out.
	Total
	27a. logical people.
	27b. feeling people.
	Total
	28a. being free to do things on the spur of the moment.
	28b. knowing well in advance what I am expected to do.
	Total

	29a. being the center of attention.
	29b. being reserved.
	Total
	30a. imagining the nonexistent.
	30b. examining details of real situations.
	Total
	31a. experiencing emotional situations.
	31b. using my abilities to analyze situations.
	Total
	32a. starting meetings at a prearranged time.
	32b. starting meetings when all are comfortable or ready.
	Total

Personal Preference Survey Scoring

Instructions: Transfer your scores for each item of each pair to the appropriate blanks in the form on the following page. Be careful to check the a and b letter to be sure you are recording scores in the right blank spaces. Then total the scores for each dimension, Enter the letter of the highest score in the space after the dimension.

E	I	S	N
1a	1b	2b	2a
5b	5a	6a	6b
9b	9a	10b	10a
13b	13a	14b	14a
17b	17a	18b	18a
21a	21b	22b	22a
25a	25b	26a	26b
29a	29b	30b	30a
Total E	Total I	Total S	Total N

T	F	J	P
3a	3b	4b	4a
7a	5a	8b	8a
11a	11b	12b	12a
15b	15a	16b	16a
19b	23a	24a	24b
27a	27b	22b	22a
25a	25b	28b	28a
31b	31a	32a	32b
Total T	Total F	Total J	Total P

J or P	E or I	S or N	T or F

Extroversion—Introversion (E or I) are complementary attitudes toward the world.

E - The Extrovert's environment is the outer world of people and things. It is what stimulates them. They are often friendly, talkative, and easy to know. They need relationships and easily express emotion. They feel pulled outward by external claims and conditions. Other people and external experiences energize them. They act first, then (maybe) reflect. Extroverts give breath to life.

I - An Introvert's essential stimulation is from within—the inner world of thoughts and reflection. Introverts often seem reserved, quiet, and feel pushed inward by external demands and perceived intrusions, but energized by inner resources and internal experiences. They reflect, then (maybe) act. Introverts give depth to life.

Sensing —Intuition (S or N) are ways of taking in information.

S - The Sensing function takes in information with five senses - seeing, hearing, smelling, touching, and tasting. They look at specific parts and pieces. They live in the present, enjoying what's here. Sensors prefer to handle practical matters. They like things that are definite and measurable. They start at the beginning and take one step at a time. They like working hands-on with the parts, to see the overall design. Sensors prefer set procedures and established routines.

N - The Intuition function processes information through an additional sixth sense or hunch. Intuitives prefer to look at patterns and relationships. They often live in the future, anticipating what might be. They like possibilities and opportunities to be inventive. They can jump anywhere and (intuitively) leap over steps. They study the overall design to see how parts fit together. Intuitives like change and variety.

Thinking—Feeling (T or F) are ways of making decisions.

T - The Thinking function decides based on logic and objective considerations. Another way to say it is that people who are thinkers decide with their head. They use logic and concern for truth and justice. They see things as an onlooker from the outside. Thinkers take a long view. They are good at analyzing plans.

F - The Feeling function decisions are based on personal subjective values. They use personal conviction and are concerned for relationships and harmony. Feeling types see things as a participant from within a situation. They take an immediate, personal view. They are typically good at understanding people.

Judging—Perceiving (J or P) tell if you prefer structure or flexibility

J - The Judging lifestyle is decisive, planned, and orderly. Judgers like to set clear limits and categories. They feel comfortable establishing closure. People with the judgment preference handle deadlines and like planning. They organize their lifestyle with definite order and structure. Life is best when it is under control.

P - The Perceiving lifestyle is flexible, adaptable, and spontaneous. Perceiving types enjoy being curious and discovering surprises. They like the freedom to explore without limits. They meet deadlines by a last-minute rush. They prefer a flexible lifestyle which means going with the flow. Experiencing life as it happens is their top preference

E - Extroversion	I - Introversion
Direct their energy and attention outward	Direct their energy and attention inward
Tuned in to external environment	Drawn to their inner world
Prefer to communicate by talking	Prefer to communicate in writing
Learn best through doing or discussing	Learn best by reflection
Have broad interests	Possess a depth of interest
Tend to speak first, reflect later	Tend to reflect before acting or speaking
Are sociable and expressive	Are private and cautious
Take initiative in work and relationships	Focus readily
S - Sensing	**N - Intuition**
Like to take information in through their senses	Want to grasp patterns and use *sixth sense*
Focus on what is real	Focus on possibilities
Value practical applications	Value imaginative insight
Are factual and concrete, notice details	Are abstract and theoretical
Observe and remember sequentially	See patterns and meanings in facts
Are present oriented	Are future-oriented
Want information step-by-step	Jump around, leap in anywhere
Trust experience	Trust inspiration
T - Thinking	**F - Feeling**
Their goal is decisions based on objective standards	Their goal is harmony, decisions based on person-centered values
Analytical	Sympathetic
Logical problem-solvers	Assess impact on people
Use cause-and-effect reasoning	Guided by personal values
Tough-minded	"Tender-hearted"
Strive for impersonal, objective truth	Strive for harmony and
Reasonable	Individual validation
Fair	Compassionate
	Accepting

J - Judging	P - Perceiving
Like closure - to have things decided	Like things loose and open to change
Want to regulate and control life	Seek to experience and understand life rather than control it
Scheduled	Flexible
Organized	Casual
Systematic	Spontaneous
Methodical	Open-ended
Plan	Adapt
Avoid last-minute stresses	Feel energized by last-minute pressures

Descriptions from Myers-Briggs Personality Types

Go back to the scoring sheet on page 85. Transfer the information here:

E or I	S or N	T or F	J or P

Match the personality type listed below to your score.

For example: If you scored higher in the I and S and F and P, the corresponding description would be **ISFP.** The description is the fourth item on this page.

ISTJ-Serious, quiet, earn success by concentration and thoroughness. Practical, orderly, matter-of-fact, logical. Realistic and dependable. See to it that everything is well organized. Take responsibility. Make up their own minds about what should be accomplished and work towards it steadily, regardless of protests or distractions.

ISTP-Cool onlookers-quiet, reserved, observing and analyzing life with detached curiosity and unexpected flashes of original humor. Usually interested in cause and effect, how and why mechanical things work, and in organizing facts based on logical principles.

ISFJ-Quiet, friendly, responsible and conscientious. Work devotedly to meet their obligations. Lend stability to any project or group. Thorough, painstaking, accurate. Their interests are usually not technical. Can be patient with necessary details. Loyal, considerate, perceptive, concerned with how other people feel.

ISFP-Retiring, quietly friendly, sensitive, kind, modest about their abilities. Shun disagreements. Do not force their opinions or values onto others. Rarely care to lead but are often loyal followers. Often relaxed about getting things done because they enjoy the present moment and do not want to spoil it by undue haste or exertion.

ESTP-Good at on-the-spot problem solving. Do not worry, enjoy whatever comes along. Like mechanical things and sports, with friends on the side. Adaptable, tolerant conservative in values. Dislike long explanations. Are best with real things that can be worked, handled, taken apart, or put together.

ESTJ-Practical, realistic, matter-of-fact, with a natural head for business or mechanics. Not interested in subjects they see no use for, but can apply themselves when necessary. Like to organize and run activities. May make good administrators, especially if they remember to consider others' feelings and points of view.

ESFJ-Warm-hearted, talkative, popular, conscientious, born cooperators, active committee members. Need harmony and may be good at creating it. Always doing something nice for someone. Work best with encouragement and praise. Main interest is in things that directly and visibly affect people's lives.

INFJ-Succeed by perseverance, originality and desire to do whatever is needed and wanted. Put their best efforts into their work. Quietly forceful, conscientious, concerned for others. Respected for their firm principles. Likely to be honored and followed for their clear convictions-how best to serve the common good.

INTJ-Usually have original minds and great drive for their own ideas and purposes. In fields that appeal to them, they have a fine power to organize a job and carry it through with or without help. Skeptical, critical, independent, determined, sometimes stubborn. Must learn to yield to less important points to win the most important.

INFP-Full of enthusiasms and loyalties, but seldom talk of these until they know you well. Care about learning, ideas, language and independent projects on their own. Undertake too much, and then somehow get it done. Friendly, but often too absorbed in what they are doing to be sociable. Little concern with possessions or physical surroundings.

INTP-Quiet and reserved. Especially enjoy theoretical or scientific pursuits. Like solving problems with logic and analysis. Usually interested mainly in ideas, with little liking for parties or small talk. Have sharply defined interests. Need careers where some strong interest can be useful.

ENFP-Warmly enthusiastic, high-spirited, ingenious, imaginative. Able to do anything that interests them. Quick with a solution for any difficulty and ready to help anyone with a problem. Often rely on their ability to improvise versus preparing in advance. Can usually find compelling reasons for whatever they want.

ENTP-Quick, ingenious, good at many things. Stimulating company, alert and outspoken. May argue for fun on either side of a question. Resourceful in solving new and challenging problems, but may neglect routine assignments. Apt to turn to one new interest after another. Skillful in finding logical reasons for what they want.

ENFJ-Responsive and responsible. Feel real concern for what others think and want and try to handle things with true regard for the other person's feelings. Can present a proposal or lead a group discussion with ease and tact. Sociable, popular, sympathetic. Responsive to praise and criticism.

ENTJ-Hearty, frank, decisive leaders in activities. Usually good in anything that requires reasoning and intelligent talk, such as public speaking. Well informed and enjoy adding to their fund of knowledge. May sometimes appear more positive and confident than their experience justifies.

- 3 - Plan

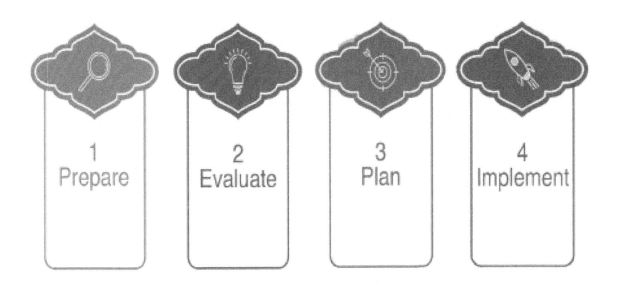

1
Prepare

2
Evaluate

3
Plan

4
Implement

What to Expect in this Section

You Are More Likely to Hit the Target if You Know What You Are Aiming At (Setting Goals for Yourself)

A successful job search mandates you set specific goals for yourself.

Research shows people who set clear and measurable goals are more likely to reach these goals. Later in this book I will provide you with specific methods for setting targets for yourself and a means of following through on them. For now, write goals you have for yourself.

Example: I want to find a job closer to home so I have more family time.

The Keys to Effective Behavior in a Job Search

The following section describes the steps you should go through as you pursue your next job. It summarizes the steps you have already taken as you completed the exercises in the earlier chapters of this book.

Self-knowledge

It is only when you know what you are best at, where your preferences lie, what you need out of work, who you work well with and which circumstances you are better off avoiding that you can make the optimum career choice.

Being empowered

Once you know what you want, you also to need to feel that you have the power to go after it. You need to see the future filled with possibilities versus the past holding you back.

Problem-solving skills

Once you know what you can offer and the energy required to pursue it, you need to have the tools to succeed. Whom do you talk to, how do you make the best presentation, and how do you overcome obstacles? Consider new paradigms. Turn lemons into lemonade.

Clear purpose

During your search, you need to stay focused and keep your eye on the goals you have set for yourself. Once you know what is important, it is easier to stay motivated. Don't paint that garage if that means you aren't pursuing your new job.

Setting priorities

Which activities have the greatest payoff? If you know networking is the method most likely to get you the job leads and information you need, does it make sense to spend most of your time answering newspaper ads or sending out mass mailings to poorly researched organizations? Always keep in mind the results you are looking for and use the methods most likely to get you what you want.

Being persistent

You want (and need) a job more than the employers and contacts you meet want (and need) for you to be hired. You need to be proactive and follow through on your objectives. People appreciate highly motivated individuals and are more likely to hire people who act as if getting the job is important to them. Remember to always be friendly and polite. The more pleasant you are to others, the more you can push.

Two-way communication skills

You need to communicate effectively by getting your ideas across and by listening carefully to others. Few things will turn someone off faster than asking a question and then ignoring the response, or, during an interview, not listening to the question asked and talking about something else.

Developing a win-win attitude

From networking to negotiating you need to see the job search process as a series of mutually beneficial activities. When you can show that you have as much to offer as you are asking for, people will respond positively. If you ask for networking leads not only should you be friendly towards your contacts but also offer to return the favor to them, or to people they know, if the need should ever arise.

Developing alliances and networking

Networking should be an enjoyable activity. It gives you a chance to strengthen relationships, meet new people, and connect with people from your past that you may not have spoken to recently. It should be an ongoing activity, not just when you are in the middle of a job search. You will know about opportunities as they develop, and people will be more likely to think of you when a new position opens.

Next are specific steps to help you with conducting a focused, efficient job search. Finally, we have techniques to help you stay motivated through the frustrations and rejections expected as part of the job search process.

Job Search Skills

The following steps are important in staying focused in your job search:

Identify job openings

Of the many methods of getting a job, we will review networking, using employment services, civil service applications, answering ads, using state and local agencies, directly contacting employers, and using temp agencies.

Evaluate job openings

What is the right job for you?

Reviewing: Can do, Will do and Right fit.

People tend to do what is comfortable, which is often what is familiar. Other people will also steer you in the direction you have already taken in the past or, what can be worse, the direction they have taken. As you go through the assessment process, keep in mind that this is an opportunity for you to target employment for which you determine you are a good match. You want a job that allows you to use your strengths, one that allows you to grow and will keep you engaged. You also want to know how likely you are to get along with customers (all jobs have customers), coworkers, and your boss. In addition, does the position support your ability to move towards the accomplishment of your life goals (self-development, education, family, friends, all in balance)? When you have tested all these factors, you can determine if a job is right for you.

Organize documents essential for employment

Deal with issues of citizenship, certifications, social security, work history, diplomas. It's easier on you if you organize any documents that you may need for your job search ahead of time. You will seem well prepared and can avoid the anxiety that can develop if you have to wait until something you need becomes available.

Prepare a resume or resumes

See section on resume development.

Fill out application forms

Take the individual profile you have filled out. It is easier to be consistent. Have a strategy about how to handle what may be problem areas such as frequent job changes or discharges. Prepare an answer for each problem area.

Written Responses

How to write a response to an ad and how to make direct, proactive written contact with an employer. Think about and specify how your strengths meet or surpass their needs.

Applying for a job by telephone

Organize your calls and do your research. Make sure you have a quiet environment to call from and are focused on the task. Prepare the key points you want to make and seek to set up a face–to–face meeting if you believe there is a potential job match.

Apply for a job on site

Check out job openings. Bring the right documents. Prepare as if they will interview you. Depending on the job you are considering, it is possible you may be interviewed immediately. While this is not how executives get hired, there are professions where this can happen. I have been present when nurses and IT professionals were interviewed as walk-ins and were given an offer on the spot.

Interview for a job.

Appearance, attitude, answering questions, showing interest. You need to look and sound appropriate for a position you are applying for. Dress in business attire. Consider appearing as you expect the interviewer would appear. You also need to understand how you can contribute to the organization so they will want to hire you. Be as prepared as you can. Try to find out who will conduct the interview and how many people will be involved. Use LinkedIn to find out about people's backgrounds. Have your resume ready and review your accomplishments. Review your research of the organization. Engage the interviewers and don't forget to smile.

Completing required test and/or screening procedures

Legal screening procedures and preparing references. Be open to and cooperative with their evaluation process. If given an aptitude test or psychological assessment, answer it honestly. While some may be "faked," if being dishonest in your answers is necessary to get the job, you probably will not be a good fit for it. Above all, take these assessments seriously. Most organizations will take the results into consideration when making a hiring decision.

Evaluating job offers

How to know if an offer will meet your needs. Go beyond the salary offered and consider if the job moves you closer to meeting your goals in your profession and in work/life balance. The clearer you are about what you offer and what you are looking for, the easier it is to make the right decision. Be prepared to negotiate to get the best deal possible. (See *Job Search Grid* regarding negotiation).

Accepting a job offer

Get written confirmation. Be clear about your responsibilities and how your performance will be measured. Now is the time to get details in writing. Don't assume; as your potential employer to clarify it in writing.

Evaluating job rejection

Learn from the experience. You should get feedback from the employer so you can do better next time.what you want to say and how you want to say it. Consider what employers are looking for and how you can develop their interest in you. Use *word cloud* to go through the job requirements and preferences listed in the job

Keeping Motivated

A job search can be an exciting adventure. You have the opportunity for new, stimulating activities, the chance to meet interesting people (and hopefully start or reinforce lifetime relationships), and the opportunity to take on new challenges. You're probably thinking, "Is he crazy? A job search is frustrating and stressful." Well, as the cliché says, you can see the glass as half full or half empty.

The way you approach the task is more than half the battle. You will have the occasion to learn a great deal about yourself, and if you are like most people, this will be the first time you have truly focused on what is important to you. Life is not a rehearsal (even though we may want to practice some behaviors); it is time to go after what you want.

Here are several useful techniques to keep motivated:

Review your personal mission statement.

Do this as often as necessary to remind you about what the job search is all about. The surer you are about your target, the more likely you will work hard to attain it.

Review, and add to, your accomplishments and skills list.

Remember all the contributions you have made to people and organizations in the past— and will make in the future.

Get a career coach/counselor.

Select someone with experience in assessment who is knowledgeable regarding occupational choices and the practical techniques that lead to success.

Always have at least two things to look forward to.

Even when you think that you just had a great second interview, it pays to have other activities in the pipeline—people change their mind, decisions get delayed. When people feel too dependent on one activity or decision, they get anxious; when they don't see their next step, they get depressed. This means schedule a series of activities such as informational interviews, networking contacts, meetings with recruiters (employment services), checking out several web sites or revisiting those contacts you haven't spoken to recently.

Take good care of yourself.

Exercise and eat well. Keep in contact with friends. Even if you are out of work and money is tight, there are lots of activities that are entertaining and cost little. You need not be "running on empty" while you are going through a major transition.

Stay as objective as possible.

While you are ultimately accountable for your behavior and need to improve your performance, you need to know people rarely return phone calls promptly (if at all). They make decisions that affect you, such as a position not being filled due to economic factors that are beyond your control.

Develop a support network.

That includes family, friends, professional acquaintances, and mentors. Not only will you get emotional support but also practical aid in advice and networking. I've known people who created a board of directors who they conferred with about the direction of their search and the effectiveness of the methods they employed.

I have met people who have tried to keep their job search a secret from those closest to them because "I didn't want to get them upset." I guarantee there is no better way of upsetting those close to you than not letting them know you are making a major decision (one which may significantly influence them) and not sharing any information with them. One outplacement client I worked with never told his family he had lost his job. He pretended that he was going to the office every day (one he no longer had), until he landed his new position. His wife and children felt betrayed—I'm not sure that the relationship ever recovered. While I am not recommending that you tell your elderly grandmother with the heart condition or your three-year-old son you are looking for a job, it is appropriate to tell a fourth grader and your parents you are changing employment. They will figure it out anyway and probably have negative fantasies if you don't tell them. One child asked his parents if this meant that he could not go to college; he was nine. Reassure them.

When you have a negative thought, challenge it.

It's common to get temporarily discouraged during a job search, especially if it takes longer than expected. People sometimes categorize an event as catastrophic that may be nothing more than a delay or temporary setback. Most of our negative thoughts are opinions, not facts. Is it really likely that "I'll never find the job I'm looking for"? Check out the assumptions that your thinking is based on. Are these assumptions sound? If you feel stuck, talk to a mentor or friend about your job search.

It's OK to be persistent, especially if you are friendly and polite.

It's a common occurrence to have someone whom you have been pursuing for weeks thank you for not giving up in trying to contact them.

7 Habits of Highly Effective Job Seekers

I was working on a large career development project (100 managers in a Fortune 50 Corporation) that entailed each individual creating a clear personal mission statement, understanding how to successfully handle the changing environment at work, understanding their strengths and creating a plan to succeed. One participant stated we must be Covey trained. I didn't know who Covey was at the time but eventually researched and understood the overlap.

Stephen R. Covey wrote *The 7 Habits of Highly Effective People*. The book examines the kinds of behaviors and attitudes that have historically been seen as leading to individual and organizational success. I strongly recommends reading this book.

Covey believes that having your life focused on being "principle centered" (acting with integrity, being a caring person) provides a compass to help you live a productive and ethical life.

The book offers many useful insights in improving one's own behavior and bettering one's relationship with others.

One particular principle is *The Emotional Bank Account.*

The premise of *The Emotional Bank Account* is that, over time, we can make deposits or withdrawals with other people regarding positive or negative behaviors and communications. This process will affect the level of trust and patience we have with each other). The following are Covey's list of productive habits (patterns of behavior).

1. Be Proactive
2. Begin with the End in Mind
3. First Things First
4. Win-Win Solutions
5. Seek First to Understand, then Be Understood
6. Synergize
7. Sharpen the Saw

I believe that each of Covey's *7 Habits* can be applied to developing a more effective job search. The following are ways to implement the *7 Habits*. After you have read each section, use the set of worksheets to help you set goals and objectives.

1. Be Proactive.

The most effective job seekers want to take the initiative in pursuing career and job opportunities. They have a sense of urgency and a belief they are in control of their fate (Internal Locus of Control). Why put off until tomorrow what they can do today if not immediately? In fact, people with this characteristic often have taken the "next step" in their career ladder before they encounter a crisis. They have developed and maintained an active network of professional alliances, are active in community and professional organizations, and often have multiple mentors. As one executive told me, "I have never looked for a job. I am always networking and keeping positive relationships. People seem to seek me out when they hear of opportunities they think match my interests." Not everyone is so fortunate, but he serves as a wonderful example. In another situation (and my first outplacement case), a recently terminated sales manager came to my office with a list of people he planned to contact. He told me how he would organize his time by contacting people in different locations explain how he would be in their area and asked for appointments. Six weeks later, having averaged almost four in- person contacts per day, he had a new position (and 25% more income).

2. Begin with the End in Mind.

One of the first activities I have my clients do, before they start their search, is to develop a Purpose or Personal Mission Statement. In examining the values and principles central to their lives and writing the goals they have for the various roles they play, clients develop much greater enthusiasm and take greater ownership of their job search activities. I also find that, while some may consider a Purpose Statement as touchy-feely, clients who have determined what is important and who take ownership for their strengths tend to maximize their income while finding their next position in less time. The Purpose Statement serves as the capstone of the assessment process. It incorporates insights gained through accomplishment analysis, personal style and interest inventories, and other commonly used assessment instruments.

How to create a Purpose Statement

A purpose statement will serve as a focus for leading a useful and satisfying life. A job or career should support the goals you select. I suggest that you use the following questions to facilitate your thinking:

- The things that I most admire in others are:
- The people who seem to get the greatest joy and are most contented are that way because:
- If I did not have to work for a living and I could do anything I wanted, I would:
- The moments I feel the greatest satisfaction are:

- My most positive qualities are:
- My most valuable actions have been:
- The things I do (or could do) that would be of the most valuable to others are:
- My fantasy about what I should really do in life is:

Write your key values and principles that you accept responsibility for and choose to live by. In other words, what is your purpose in life?

List your Purpose Statement in the worksheet on pages 106-107.

Roles and Goals

We play a variety of roles in our lives regarding different relationships and circumstances such as parent, child, spouse, friend, employer, community member, and so on. For each of these roles we develop, consciously or unconsciously, a variety of goals. In the long run it is important to have a balance in our lives. What are the important roles in your life and the goals you have for each?

3. First Things First

Putting *First Things First* means prioritizing and managing your activities.

Plan to follow through on job search activities that are most likely to have a positive payoff.

- Too many clients become discouraged and burned out, complaining about how much time they have spent in their job search. They feel they have nothing to show for their hard work.

- In almost every case they have either failed to set meaningful goals or pursued job search activities that are less likely to have a positive impact.

- Perhaps they have answered dozens of want ads or send out "shotgun" mailings instead of pursuing more productive avenues in their job search.

Covey talks about distinguishing between that which is ***important*** and that which seems, or is, ***urgent***. Urgent activities may, on the surface, appear to be pressing, like beginning your search activities immediately after losing your job or calling all your friends for help. Unless you have determined what you want and have developed a strategy to get it, these activities are urgent but are not especially important.

Being well-prepared is sometimes overlooked by those who feel desperate, and this usually leads to a longer search period and unnecessary frustration. The job seeker who considers which activities have the greatest impact in attaining their goals will be much more effective in the long run.

4. Win–Win Solutions

The job searches that get the best results are those where people see themselves as part of a series of positive relationships. Each person you meet is a resource of information and potential job leads. You should offer to become part of their work network, offering to be of help to them, their friends or family, if the need ever arises. Through a spirit of cooperation that people tend to make the most progress.

Covey advocates creating an *emotional bank account.* He describes how people should make *deposits* with others, providing support, acting cooperatively, and doing favors for others; all of these *deposits* build up a positive relationship over a period of time. This process sets the stage for the positive social / job network that facilitates an effective job search. Now is always the time to build these relationships. Your deposits will pay off with considerable interest.

A win-win approach also is the most successful when you are negotiating your offer. To start a job after an adversarial negotiation is likely to cast a pall over the future relationship. You want the employment agreement to be seen as the beginning of a partnership, a cooperative venture. If you are able to force an employer to give you more than they think is fair, their expectations may surpass your ability to perform. They may harbor resentment and never fully support you. Wise employers will treat you with respect and fairness. Otherwise, they may find an employee who is resentful, less than committed, and more likely to leave at the earliest opportunity.

Win-win brings people together in supportive and beneficial ways. We live in an interdependent world, and successful relationships are built on a win-win philosophy.

5. Seek First to Understand, Then Be Understood

An important skill to use in a job search is the ability to listen to others. You only learn while you are listening, not when you are speaking. When you listen, people feel you respect their opinion.

One of the most difficult things in communicating with others is hearing another person's point of view. Appreciating and understanding the other person's views before trying to express your own viewpoint is critical in relationships. Seeking to understand others first allows you to act from a position of knowledge and to gain empathy. Empathy develops trust and the likelihood of coming up with creative, win-win solutions.

- Think of situations where empathic listening might improve relationships.
- What benefits might come from seeking to understand others first in your job search?

Communicating with Others

- Focus your communication

- Decide what message you want to send.

- Be consistent; don't send contradictory or mixed messages.

- Establish rapport. Seek to develop a positive relationship and understand the other person's point of view. Put the person at ease.

- Reflect back your understanding of their thoughts, feelings and behavior.

- Is the other person ready to listen to you?

State the purpose of your communication

- Keep it simple.

- Present your points one at a time.

- Give them in a logical order.

- Leave out irrelevancies.

Ask for, and listen to, the other person's response

- Use open-ended questions and feedback.

- Make sure the other person understands your point of view.

- Decide on and get agreement about actions to be taken.

- There are always next steps. Follow through and get closure.

6. Synergy

Synergy is the process of making the whole greater than the sum of its parts. Through interaction with others you become more effective in problem solving. You can use the creativity of your contact network. The people who make up your support network can provide feedback on your goals, make suggestions on increasing your positive impact on others and give you emotional support.

Remember the "board of directors" mentioned earlier that advise and suggest direction through their job search (sort of group mentoring). The group is comprised of individuals the job candidate respects and relates to, in some fashion, and are involved the industries and functions that the job seeker is interested in pursuing.

When two or more people work together to understand something, they can create a situation referred to as synergy. We can discover things together that we might not have alone. Synergy means one plus one can equal three or more. Such focused teamwork stimulates new alternatives and creates a context for mutual support that benefits everyone. Relationships that join people of different styles and diverse backgrounds together are opportunities for synergy. The more people you can enlist in your job search, the easier it will be.

When people's awareness of the mutual benefits of synergy overcomes their fears of others' differences (or potential rejection), they move to a new level of problem solving.

7. Sharpen the Saw

A job search can take a lot of energy. You need to stay focused and act. You want to make a positive impression on others. To feel competent and capable of making things happen for yourself, you need to be healthy and connected to the sources of energy that invigorate you.

To be truly effective we all need to have a healthy balance in our lives. By taking care of our various needs and maintaining balance, we protect ourselves from undue stress and burnout. A job search can be stressful. Make sure to take care of yourself.

7 Habits of Highly Effective Job Seekers Worksheets

The worksheets that begin on the next page provide an opportunity for you to respond to the *7 Habits* discussed in this section.

Each question or set of questions will help you in developing a road map to assist in your job search.

1. Be Proactive *In what ways can you become more proactive in your search?*

1.

2.

3.

4.

5.

6.

7.

2. Begin with the End in Mind *Focus on your life goals. Imagine that you are celebrating your 100th birthday and that all your family, friends, and coworkers are there to give testimony to the person you have been throughout your life. What would you like them to say about you? Have you lived the life to justify these complementary words? If not, what do you need to do differently?*

I would like them to say

I feel I have not lived the life they described because:

If you do not agree with their statements, what could you do differently?

Purpose Statement:

The things that I most admire in others are:

The people who seem to get the greatest joy and are most contented are that way because:

If I did not have to work for a living and I could do anything I wanted, I would:

The moments I feel the greatest satisfaction are:

My most positive qualities are:

My most valuable actions have been:

The things I do (or could do) that would be of the most valuable to others are:

My fantasy about what I should really do in life is:

| |
| |
| |
| |

List the key values and principles that you accept responsibility for and choose to live by. What is your purpose in life?

| |
| |
| |
| |

Roles and Goals:

Important Role:

| 1. Goal |
| 2. Goal |
| 3. Goal |

Important Role:

| 1. Goal |
| 2. Goal |
| 3. Goal |

Important Role:

| 1. Goal |
| 2. Goal |
| 3. Goal |

Important Role:

1. Goal

2. Goal

3. Goal

3. First Things First

What are the most important activities to meet the goals in your job search?

Which of these should be ongoing to maintain your career development?

4. Win-Win Solutions

Where could you apply a win-win approach in your job search activities?

5. Seek First to Understand, Then Be Understood   Think of situations where empathic listening might improve relationships. What benefits might come from seeking to understand other first in your job search?

6. Synergy In what ways could synergy help you in your job search?

7. Sharpen the Saw How can you:

Build strength and endurance through nutrition, exercise and rest.(Physical)

1.

2.

3.

4.

5.

Exercise your spiritual self (our search for meaning and connection) through inspirational literature, meditation or prayer, and through spending time with nature. (Spiritual)

1.

2.

3.

4.

5.

Life-long learning through reading, writing and taking time to think. (Mental)
1.
2.
3.
4.
5.
Develop healthy emotional relationships. Covey refers to making deposits in others emotional bank accounts. (Social-Emotional)
1.
2.
3.
4.
5.

Developing a Job Search Strategy

Careful planning and follow through can decrease the time to find the right job. You need to answer the following questions.

Exactly what job or jobs are you looking for?

Base your search on your understanding on what you can do, want to do, will do and what's available. No job is perfect so prioritize the most important factors. Research available employment opportunities. Are the kinds of position you want abundant or are they very rare? Do you want to relocate/are you willing to relocate? How much money do you want to make/need to make? Are you targeting a job that you qualify for now or will you need to take several steps to get there?

Are you prepared to make the best impression possible?

If you have not been carefully preparing yourself for a job search on an ongoing basis, give thought to giving the preparation adequate time before you try to implement a plan. You cannot be totally prepared in a couple of hours or days (two weeks would be better). Not preparing properly usually means missed opportunities and outright mistakes leading to a longer job search.

How much time are you going to devote to your job search?

If you are unemployed, it makes sense to consider your job search as a full-time job. By maintaining an active job search you build momentum. You should get energy from talking to people and are more likely to be rewarded. If you need additional motivation think about the increase in your income by getting a job sooner.

How much time will you devote to each job search activity?

Ask yourself what activities have the biggest return on investment. You do not want to ignore viable job search options, nor do you want to waste time on activities that aren't very productive. Most jobs come about through some form of networking so plan to spend a significant amount of time doing some form of networking. That can include reaching out to people through websites, phone calls and face-to-face meetings.

What are the best methods for getting the type of job you want?

Many authors refer to the *hidden job market* as if someone is trying to keep a secret from you. There are many ways of getting a job, and to be most effective you need to consider what combination of approaches will probably be most effective for you.

Here are seven ways to make yourself known to a potential employer:

1. Networking.

Networking works for everyone, (as long as you give it a chance). All the employers I interviewed mentioned networking as a significant source for their hiring and, of equal importance, the primary method that the respondents used in finding employment for themselves. Networking is the single most effective way for most people to find a job.

2. Utilizing an Employment Service.

Employment services work with a wide variety of positions. They work for employers to fill both temporary positions and full-time jobs. While they tend to fill more hourly types of employment, their services also include many types of technical positions such as nursing and information technology. Some firms specialize in placing highly trained individuals for short-term assignments.

3. Contacting Recruiters.

Recruiters work for companies to fill positions. They may be given assignments that make them the most likely inroad to certain positions.

4. Answering Ads in Newspapers and on the Internet.

While want ads are a significant source of jobs, this method will put you in competition with numerous people answering the same ad.

5. Direct Contact with Employers.

You decide who you want to work for and develop an approach to meet the appropriate person who can hire you. This can be done through a combination of activities such as writing letters, making telephone calls, and networking. Sometimes, you can simply go to an organization's employment office and fill out an application. This method is not recommended, however, for potential CEOs.

6. Placing Your Own Ad.

Ads in a newspaper or journal advertising your services in "employment wanted" ads can bring you and your skills to the attention of prospective employers. Sometimes, these ads can be placed for free.

7. Getting on the Civil Service Register.

The Federal, State, and Municipal governments are large employers with a wide variety of positions. Often a test is required to qualify for a position (although the test can sometimes be an interview).

Once you have chosen the means you will use to get a job, you need to develop your implementation plan. How much time will you devote to each activity? You should constantly monitor your activities to ensure that you are doing what will be most effective.

4 - Implement

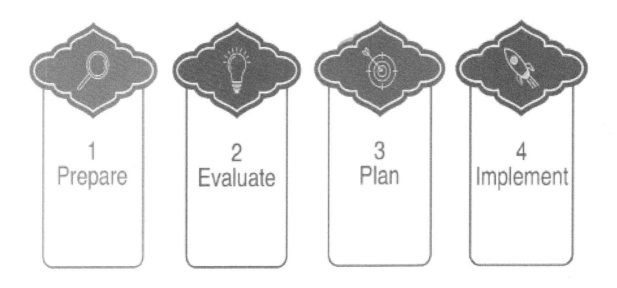

What to Expect in this Section

Employment Applications

In most cases, you will need to fill out an application. Much of the information will be available in your resume but applications often require additional details (street addresses, phone numbers, names of supervisors and their contact information) or the reason you left a position. It pays to collect this information before you need it.

- Be honest on an application. Misrepresenting your education or work experience is cause for immediate dismissal. Ironically, many people are only found out when they are about to receive promotions.
- Read and fill out the application carefully. It does not impress people if there are mistakes.
- That does not mean that you can't phrase things in a positive way, such as the reason you left a job.
- Do not be critical of past employers. Most people will consider the possibility you may be critical of them, too, if the job does not work out.
- Do not lie about past compensation. You may decide how to present information such as salary, lumping salary with bonuses, or talking about your total compensation package. In some circumstances, you may even wish to leave specific salary off the application: do this judiciously. In such cases you might write that you would like to discuss the past salary information with the interviewer.
- If asked on the application about your desired income, you are better off to write that you are flexible. It's often possible to learn about their salary range through a little research or networking. If you must put down desired salary, remember that being unreasonably high will rule you out of consideration; a low number may be what they expect you will accept.
- It is possible that an application may contain illegal questions such as race, marital status, or number of children. You do not have to answer these questions (but may not be offered the job.) An application differs from a government form that tracks applicants to insure there is no bias in hiring. It is appropriate to answer those questions.
- If an application requests information regarding your health, keep in mind you do not have to share information about health issues that do not affect performance.

APPLICATION FOR EMPLOYMENT
(Pre-Employment Questionnaire) (An Equal Opportunity Employer)

PERSONAL INFORMATION

DATE _____

NAME _____   SOCIAL SECURITY NUMBER _____

              LAST   FIRST   MIDDLE

PRESENT ADDRESS _____

              STREET   CITY   STATE   ZIP

PERMANENT ADDRESS _____

              STREET   CITY   STATE   ZIP

PHONE NO. _____   ARE YOU 18 YEARS OR OLDER?   Yes ☐   No ☐

ARE YOU PREVENTED FROM LAWFULLY BECOMING EMPLOYED
IN THIS COUNTRY BECAUSE OF VISA OR IMMIGRATION STATUS?   Yes ☐ _____   No ☐ _____

EMPLOYMENT DESIRED

POSITION _____   DATE YOU CAN START _____   SALARY DESIRED _____

ARE YOU EMPLOYED NOW? _____   IF SO MAY WE INQUIRE OF YOUR PRESENT EMPLOYER? _____

EVER APPLIED TO THIS COMPANY BEFORE? _____   WHERE? _____   WHEN? _____

REFERRED BY _____

EDUCATION	NAME AND LOCATION OF SCHOOL	*NO OF YEARS ATTENDED	*DID YOU GRADUATE?	SUBJECTS STUDIED
GRAMMAR SCHOOL				
HIGH SCHOOL				
COLLEGE				
TRADE, BUSINESS OR CORRESPONDENCE SCHOOL				

GENERAL

SUBJECTS OF SPECIAL STUDY OR RESEARCH WORK _____

SPECIAL SKILLS _____

ACTIVITIES: (CIVIC ATHLETIC ETC.) _____

EXCLUDE ORGANIZATIONS, THE NAME OF WHICH INDICATES THE RACE, CREED. SEX. AGE, MARITAL STATUS, COLOR OR NATION OF ORIGIN OF ITS MEMBERS.

U. S MILITARY OR NAVAL SERVICE _____   RANK _____   PRESENT MEMBERSHIP IN NATIONAL GUARD OR RESERVES _____

*This form has been revised to comply with the provisions of the Americans with Disabilities Act
and the final regulations and interpretive guidance promulgated by the EEOC on July 26. 1991.

TOPS FORM 3285 (92-8)   (CONTINUED ON OTHER SIDE)   LITHO IN U.S.A.

(Side markings: LAST, FIRST, MIDDLE)

FORMER EMPLOYERS (LIST BELOW LAST THREE EMPLOYERS, STARTING WITH LAST ONE FIRST).

DATE MONTH AND YEAR	NAME AND ADDRESS OF EMPLOYER	SALARY	POSITION	REASON FOR LEAVING
FROM				
TO				
FROM				
TO				
FROM				
TO				
FROM				
TO				

WHICH OF THESE JOBS DID YOU LIKE BEST?

WHAT DID YOU LIKE MOST ABOUT THIS JOB?

REFERENCES: GIVE THE NAMES OF THREE PERSONS NOT RELATED TO YOU, WHOM YOU HAVE KNOWN AT LEAST ONE YEAR.

	NAME	ADDRESS	BUSINESS	YEARS ACQUAINTED
1				
2				
3				

THE FOLLOWING STATEMENT APPLIES IN: MARYLAND & MASSACHUSETTS. [Fill in name of state.]
IT IS UNLAWFUL IN THE STATE OF _____ TO REQUIRE OR ADMINISTER A LIE DETECTOR TEST AS A CONDITION OF EMPLOYMENT OR CONTINUED EMPLOYMENT. AN EMPLOYER WHO VIOLATES THIS LAW SHALL BE SUBJECT TO CRIMINAL PENALTIES AND CIVIL LIABILITY.

Signature of Applicant

IN CASE OF EMERGENCY NOTIFY

NAME   ADDRESS   PHONE NO.

"I CERTIFY THAT ALL THE INFORMATION SUBMITTED BY ME ON THIS APPLICATION IS TRUE AND COMPLETE, AND I UNDERSTAND THAT IF ANY FALSE INFORMATION, OMISSIONS, OR MISREPRESENTATIONS ARE DISCOVERED, MY APPLICATION MAY BE REJECTED AND, IF I AM EMPLOYED, MY EMPLOYMENT MAY BE TERMINATED AT ANY TIME.
IN CONSIDERATION OF MY EMPLOYMENT, I AGREE TO CONFORM TO THE COMPANY'S RULES AND REGULATIONS, AND I AGREE THAT MY EMPLOYMENT AND COMPENSATION CAN BE TERMINATED, WITH OR WITHOUT CAUSE, AND WITH OR WITHOUT NOTICE, AT ANY TIME, AT EITHER MY OR THE COMPANY'S OPTION. I ALSO UNDERSTAND AND AGREE THAT THE TERMS AND CONDITIONS OF MY EMPLOYMENT MAY BE CHANGED, WITH OR WITHOUT CAUSE, AND WITH OR WITHOUT NOTICE, AT ANY TIME BY THE COMPANY. I UNDERSTAND THAT NO COMPANY REPRESENTATIVE, OTHER THAN IT'S PRESIDENT, AND THEN ONLY WHEN IN WRONG AND SIGNED BY THE PRESIDENT, HAS ANY AUTHORITY TO ENTER INTO ANY AGREEMENT FOR EMPLOYMENT FOR ANY SPECIFIC PERIOD OF TIME, OR TO MAKE ANY AGREEMENT CONTRARY TO THE FOREGOING.

DATE   SIGNATURE

DO NOT WRITE BELOW THIS LINE

INTERVIEWED BY: DATE:

REMARKS:

NEATNESS   ABILITY

HIRED: ☐ Yes ☐ No   POSITION   DEPT.

SALARY/WAGE   DATE REPORTING TO WORK

APPROVED: 1.   2.   3
EMPLOYMENT MANAGER   DEPT. HEAD   GENERAL MANAGER

This form has been designed to strictly comply with State and Federal fair employment practice laws prohibiting employment discrimination. This Application for Employment Form is sold for general use throughout the United States. TOPS assumes no responsibility for the inclusion in said form of any questions which, when asked by the Employer of the Job Applicant, may violate State and/or Federal Law.

Resumes

What is a Resume?

A good resume is important to your marketing campaign because:

1. Creating a resume organizes your thinking and shows how your experience supports your objective. Therefore, it helps you to express yourself more effectively on interviews.
2. It focuses on where you want to go, not where you came from. A resume should never mislead; it should target the positions and organizations you want to work for. Do this by emphasizing the accomplishments that are most similar to the needs of the job sought and use the vocabulary with which they are most comfortable.
3. Some people you will meet may be uncomfortable without a written guide. This will be especially true if your interviewer is insufficiently prepared. It is an unfortunate fact of life that and many people who interview have never been trained to do so.
4. It provides a good document to leave behind or attach to a follow-up note. It reinforces the impression you made, and can be shared with others in the company.
5. It provides documentation for a third-party spokesperson. A search firm or employment agency can forward your resume to a prospective employer for review.
6. It may open doors as you build a network of contacts.
7. A resume is a living document that should target specific jobs and match the stated needs of a particular employer. That means you may end up creating many resumes (or at least minor variations of a main resume) to best communicate your value.

Key Elements of a Resume

Heading

Identifying information, including your name, address, home and office telephone numbers and email address should head the first page in a balanced, pleasant layout.

The Objective (optional)

A clear statement, neither too specific nor too broad, states your employment objective. If you want to be considered for many positions you need to avoid it. You don't want to be pigeonholed to one title (unless it is the only position you want to be considered for, such as CEO). You should also be aware that various organizations may have different titles for the same function; a brief description may be better than a title. I usually recommend that your objective be put in the cover letter for a given position, where it can be more specific.

Summary

The next section of the action resume is the summary. The summary supports your objective—why you can do what your objective states you want to do. You may choose not to have a separate objective but instead to write your summary so that the objective will be clear. The summary should include a short statement regarding work history and relevant experience, any special skills you may have, mention of your education (if it stands out), and work-related personality characteristics. The more experience you have in your chosen field, the more you can emphasize that experience. Where you have little experience, you can describe your education, training, motivation or personal characteristics.

Examples:

- 4 years managerial experience that includes finance, sales training and supervision.

- Extensive experience in the administration of a not-for profit organization with 75 employees. Held responsibility for meeting budget, maintaining facility and supervising all areas of human resources

- Recent graduate of 4-year nursing program

- Hard working, dependable individual familiar with all components of Microsoft Office

- Have met or exceeded sales quotas in each of the past 5 years

Experience

The next part of the resume deals with employment history. You can also highlight volunteer positions that have significantly contributed to your ability to contribute to a future employer (such as President of a civic organization). Remember, the resume is a marketing/promotional piece, and only those things that enhance your strengths should be included. Anything that would detract should be omitted. As in all things, at no time should you falsify any information on a resume; it just doesn't work, and it seriously jeopardizes others' perception of your integrity once the falsehood is discovered (and eventually it will be).

The experience sections should first state the most recent or highest title in your most recent position, followed by the name of the company, location by city and state only, and years employed, for instance 1978-1981.

Do not give total number of months or years, or provide month-specific dates; this may set up an "is all the time accounted for?" mentality that could detract from the attention given your accomplishments. Then give a brief job description, emphasizing the strengths mentioned in your objective. Do not provide details of positions held more than fifteen years ago; simply summarize the nature of this early experience. Providing details will either show low-level experience or may suggest that you have not made much progress if the early experience was at a higher level. Example of such a summary:

Examples:

- Project Manager, ASC Co., Kansas City, MO (1975-Present)
- Directed a team of 30 professionals to design, build, and maintain a production facility that was cited in the 1980 annual report as the company's most productive plant.
- Twelve years in positions of increasing responsibility in sales and marketing.

Accomplishments/Results

The next part of the resume deals with accomplishments. In a chronological format resume the accomplishment will follow the brief description of each position held. The purpose of this section is to present results to further support the strengths cited in the objective/ summary. The accomplishments should:

1. Identify the problem or situation prior to your involvement;
2. Use action verbs to define what you did and what resulted;
3. Illustrate the significance or dimension of the accomplishment in quantifiable terms, e.g. dollars, people, percentages.

Examples:

- Planned construction of an industrial facility for a real-estate developer which realized a $60,000 net savings in projected construction costs.
- Developed a promotional fund-raising campaign for a local chapter of a nationally recognized youth group that provided contributions exceeding $30,000, three times the previous record.

Make sure the accomplishments strongly and directly support the objective.

Education

Educational background, where given, should be stated simply: highest degree first, followed by major, name of school and date. Then list prior degrees, if any. High schools should be shown only if there is no college level training indicated, and only if it is relevant to the objective. Other training, certificates, or educational attainments should also be shown if they provide significant support to the objective.

Other Relevant Data (optional)

This can include memberships, language skills and personal data that support the objective. One should usually leave out explicit indications of religious affiliation, political orientation, or controversial activities. I had a client who wanted to put down that he did skydiving, white water rafting and full contact karate. I felt too many employers would think he was a bad insurance risk. Use this category only if these activities substantially contribute to your value as an employee, for instance if you had a leadership position or you picked up a marketable skill.

Choice of Resume Format

Two formats have been found to be effective for most job seekers:

Chronological Resume

The first of these is the chronologically arranged resume that defines your objective, summarizes your experience, and then describes each job in reverse chronological sequence. For this format, you should first describe your responsibilities and then give evidence (through illustrative accomplishments) of how well you carried out those responsibilities. The chronologically arranged resume is normally the right choice for a person seeking a similar or more senior position of the same type and in the same or a closely related industry.

Functional Resume

The second main format is the functionally arranged resume that defines your objective, summarizes your experience, and then illustrates the key functional capabilities by means of accomplishments that are important in the type of job described in the objective. This arrangement can be used to show one's ability to perform a somewhat different job or to handle the requirements of a position in a different industry or to dimish gaps in your work hisotry. Following the functional outline, you then briefly provides a chronology of your employers, positions, and dates, so that the reader can readily see your career history and place the accomplishments in context.

There is a lot of potential help in creating a resume. Google Docs, Word Templates, Indeed, CareerBuilder, Monster, State Departments of Labor and other sites provide templates for resume creation. If you use their models, remember, your resume will only be as good as your development of your message. And your resume must be targeted to the specific employer.

Resume Language

- Resume language should be specific rather than general, and active or action oriented rather than passive.

- Information about your past experience and accomplishments is relevant only if it illustrates your potential contribution in the area of your job objective.

- Give results whenever possible, either in absolute terms such "saved $40,000.by eliminating waste" or relative terms, "doubled the number of new leads."

Resume Worksheet

| **Your Name** |
| **Address** |
| **Telephone(s)** |
| **Email** |
| **Objective** (Optional. I don't recommend): Make certain it is basen on your greatest strengths. Don't make it so narrow that it rules you out of a position you might want. Remember, you are answering the question: "What do you want to do? |
| |
| |
| |
| |
| |
| **Summary** An overview of your career (e.g. years of experience- in_____ and _____). The question you're answering here is: "What makes you think you can do that?" Your summary should be supported by your accomplishments. You can use word cloud (sample job descriptions to ensure that you have used the most relevant key words |
| |
| |
| |
| |
| |
| |
| |
| |
| |
| |

Accomplishments List contributions that you are most proud of (25-30 words maximum). In each, you should answer at least one of the following:

- How much money have you saved your organization?
- By what percent did you increase sales/output/productivity?
- Using action words, how much did you increase or improve those things that can't always be measured (morale, public relations, etc.)?
- What were the bottom line results for your firm or organization based on your important contributions?

IMPORTANT: List specific contributions or achievements here, not areas of competence or job duties.

1
2
3
4
5
6
7
8

Experience List in chronological order the different jobs you have had (starting with your most recent position). List employers, locations, titles, brief job descriptions and dates

Education List degrees and dates as well as special achievements, awards, honors, and contributions if applicable. Also list all special training courses or seminars you have attended.

Professional organizations/clubs

Personal List any relevant information that supports your objectives or adds dimensions you want people to know about.

Sample Resume (Chronological)

Stephen L. Davis
123 Anystreet
Yourtown, Ohio 12345

Phone: 213 213 2814
S.Davis@gmail.com

Summary

Five years of increasing responsibility in national TV commercial productions, with budgets exceeding $1million. Successful at managing 25+ people of varying temperaments during high pressure, deadline-driven situations. Self motivated, with superb communication skills. Outstanding at acclimating to new concepts quickly. Have written and sold scripts for film and television.

Experience

The AdMan   Los Angeles, CA   1998-present   Project Manager
- Spots include Coke, Nike, Kentucky Fried Chicken
- Supervise production teams ranging from 6-15 people
- Mediate shooting schedule between Advertising Agency and Director
- Recruit and hire camera department, extras, lighting unit
- Monitor costs and schedules for locations and actors
- Responsible for pre and post production purchases

Commercials, Inc.   Los Angeles, CA   1995-1998   Production Coordinator
- Spots included Pepsi, Microsoft, and Canon
- Managed purchases, usages, returns of camera and set equipment
- Budgeted transportation expenses/hours with Teamsters Union
- Delegated pre-production tasks to office team

Productions, Inc. Los Angeles, CA 1994-1995 Production Associate
- "In Living Color"; "The Golden Girls"
- Allocated in-house office finances
- Drafted daily itineraries for writers/director

Education

University of California at Los Angeles
Advanced Graduate Writing Program
University of Iowa
BA English 1991 Dean's list. Coeditor, Hawkeye Yearbook

Computer skills:

Mac and IBM Compatible

Chronological Format Resume (one or two pages based on experience)

Name
Address
Telephone
Summary Three to five sentences providing an overview of your qualifications for the position that you want.
Experience Start with your present position and work backwards. Focus on the last five to ten years, and emphasize the accomplishments that support your objective and summary.
Organization name Location (city and state)
Dates
Title
Brief statement of responsibility
Accomplishments List the results of up to six accomplishments. Be concise

Previous position
Organization name Location (city and state)
Dates
Title
Brief statement of responsibility
Accomplishments List the results of up to six accomplishments. Be concise
Repeat the process for the next position. In general, you will want to emphasize your most recent jobs on your resume. Remember to think in terms of which jobs and accomplishments will create the closest match between you and the job you want.
Education Follow experience with education and any specific training that applies. (Omit high school if you have college or other advanced forms of education.)
Institution
Degree/Dates
Institution
Degree/Dates
Institution
Degree/Dates

Personal Interests If you have room you can mention activities such as volunteer activities or membership in organizations that enhance your credentials.

Sample Resume (Functional)

Education

PhD, Biology, University of Notre Dame; 1971
MS, Biology, Michigan State University; 1968;
BA, Biology, Earlham College; 1963;
Teachers College, Columbia University, 1985-86
Computers and Education Program (30 Hrs.),

Highlights of Qualifications

- 10 years PC Desktop and LAN support.

- 10 years PC relational database development and support in MSAccess97, Clipper, and Lotus Approach.

- 10 years Software support Windows95/98/NT, MSOffice95/97/2000 and other software such as (insert latest).

- 8 years supervising computer support team for SATA (4 Years) and TAT (4 years) contracts. Managed the use of ARC view GIS, WEB site development and implementation, and GPS use.

- 8 years working with state and local Hazardous Materials Information Management systems within EPA Region 3, especially the State of Delaware Hazardous Information Management Committee and the Commonwealth of Virginia's Department of Emergency Services. Consulted with many local emergency planners and responders in every state within Region 3 on implementation of EPCRA information systems.

- 10 years of computer and emergency responders training including 40-hr OSHA HAZWOPER, 8-hr refresher, 16-hr operations, 4-hr Hospital Decon, and 16/24 hr. CAMEO course.

- 30 years teaching experience at all levels. College, High School, Middle School, and Adult classes.

- 8 years of additional relevant computer experience; computer hardware and software support in schools, development and implementation of computer curriculum.

- Experience in statistical analysis for multimedia sampling, chemical safety audits, and risk analysis.

Experience

Roy F. Weston, Inc., Somewhere, NJ   1989-Present   Computer Officer (1991- present)

- Designed, setup and maintain Novell 4.1 Network LAN for SATA office.

- Responsible for PC software and hardware support for SATA contract.

- Developed and taught over 30 CAMEO courses in every state in EPA Region III. Attended all CAMEO workshops and was an instructor at CAMEO99 in Phoenix.

- Taught First Responder courses 40 Hr. OHSA, Operations, Awareness, and Hospital Decon courses

- Provided computer support for SATA Project Officer especially with Automated TDD Generating System.

- Supervised SATA support for Emergency Response Notification System and Regional Response Room coverage.

- Developed, programmed and maintained Information Systems for EPA data, i.e. Oil Spill Penalty Tracking System (Spillpen), SATA Technical Direction Document Information Management, Time Management and reporting system.

- Consulted with states (VA, DE, and MD) in EPA Region III on electronic reporting and data storage/retrieval for EPCRA (SARA Title III) requirements.

- Presented workshops on Information Management of Hazardous Materials using CAMEO and other systems at Region III CEPP Conference (1999, 1997, 1995), PA HazMat Conference (1997), and VA HazMat Conference (1996,1997,1998, 1999).

Programmer Analyst   1989-1991

- Provided PC support for hardware and software under TAT contract.

- Using dBase III+ programmed databases for sites including mail merge letters for residences.

- Maintained ATGS and SIMS information systems for TAT contract.

- Taught First Responder Awareness and Operations courses.

Private School, Somewhere, NJ   1979-1989   Computer/Biology Teacher

- Started Computer program at school and setup computer room.

- Planned and implemented evening Adult Computer classes and Summer Computer Camp.

- Developed advanced courses in Biology and computer programming.

Private College, Somewhere, Ohio   1973-1979

- Associate Professor and Chairman, Biology Dept.

- Responsible for curriculum upgrade and implementation of faculty evaluation and development program.

US Peace Corps,   Somewhere in Africa   1971-1973

- Head of Biology Department and tutor in teacher training program.

Certification:

- NJ Permanent Teaching Certificate (Biology)
- Microsoft Certified Systems Engineer (MCSE)

Functional Format Resume Worksheet

Use a functional format resume if you want to change direction from your previous position or if there is a gap in your employment history. The first page emphasizes functional expertise, and the second page lists where you have worked and your educational achievements.

Name
Address
Telephone
Summary Three to five sentences providing an overview of your qualifications for the position that you want
Functional area (such as sales, new product development, MIS, equipment specialization)
Accomplishment
Accomplishment
Accomplishment

Next functional area
Accomplishment
Accomplishment
Second Page
Organization
Location
Dates
Title
Organization
Location
Dates
Title
Education
Institution
Degree
Dates
Institution
Degree
Dates
Institution
Degree
Dates

References

Preparing Your References

When deciding to hire an employee, most employers will check references before making a final offer. In general, they are looking to confirm their positive impression of the job candidate and to find out if there are any problem areas they might have missed. Some employers put considerable effort in learning about a potential employee (credit checks and speaking to each reference listed). Others are only interested that you have someone listed as a reference. It is always better to be prepared for a thorough check.

Each of your job-related references should be a professional who will provide accurate, objective information about you. Before your first interview you should decide on the people you want to use for references and discuss with these individuals what they will say about you. First, it is polite to ask permission to use someone as a reference. Secondly, by reviewing what they will say about you, it can reduce the likelihood of getting any unpleasant surprises. Thirdly, you can get important feedback about how you were viewed. Finally, this discussion is an opportunity to get networking leads.

If your application calls for a personal reference, choose carefully. Again, be sure to ask if this person is willing to serve as a reference for you and if he or she feels comfortable in presenting you in a positive light.

Normally, you will want to list your last few supervisors. If there was a significant problem with a supervisor, you want to choose your supervisor's boss or an upwardly diagonal relationship. If you do not use an immediate past supervisor, you should be prepared with a plausible explanation as to why not, and a suitable substitute.

In addition to past employers, other references can include people who were customers and people who know you well from the community. This would not include relatives or friends who did not also have a professional relationship with you.

Most companies now have a policy that references should not be given out. The only information sanctioned is dates of employment and titles. While many people will ignore this "no references" policy because they like a previous employee, it is possible that someone you were counting on may need to refuse.

Getting positive references can make the difference in being offered a position or being an also ran. And, in some cases, a negative reference can sabotage someone moving on in their career. There was a situation several years ago where a Vice President in a large corporation decided to tell off his boss in public after learning about his impending downsizing. The word got out about what he did and he had trouble getting work for over a year. It's best to try not to burn bridges; you may need these work-related relationships in the future.

Be aware that our lives are more exposed to the public than ever before. If you are active on social media, you can be researched by anyone. Comments made, pictures posted, causes supported, can all be seen. If you are seen as holding extreme views, or acting immaturely, it can prevent you from being hired. Consider deactivating Facebook (or similar sites), if you might be vulnerable.

Many employers run credit checks. Pay down outstanding bills if at all possible.

Get conviction expunged, if at all possible. There are jobs where you have to pass a security clearance or a drug charge will block you. Sometimes, you can make these problems disappear.

Reference Worksheet

Use this worksheet to list the confirmed information regarding your references. Make sure that you have up-to-date information. Always bring a printed copy of your references to an interview.

Title	Name	
Address		
City	State	ZIP
Telephone Numbers		
Email		
How do you know this individual?		
Title	Name	
Address		
City	State	ZIP
Telephone Numbers		
Email		

Cover Letters

The purpose of a cover letter is to help generate a favorable reply to information you are sending to a contact or prospective employer. It should:

- Introduce you and your background

- State the purpose of your contact

- Clarify your objective (especially if your resume does not have an objective)

- Act as a sales letter intended to show the reader that you have something of value to contribute

Make sure that your letter addresses these three key purposes:

1. Why you are writing

2. What you have to offer

3. What you would like to happen

To ensure that the cover letter is effective:

- If sent by mail, use good quality bond paper (that matches your resume paper) Address your letter to a specific person and title. If you are not sure about whom to send it to, do some research. You can always call the company to find out.

- Make sure that the cover letter is appropriate to the job. With the ability to store cover letters on websites like CareerBuilder, you may try to use the same letter for different jobs. Always make sure the letter is targeted to the position.

- Write in a style that is friendly, business oriented, and direct. Proofread carefully, and ask someone else to proofread, too, so that your letter will be free of any errors. Use action verbs. Do not simply repeat what's in your resume. Use this opportunity to deal directly with the specific needs or concerns of the person you are writing to.

- Limit your letter to one page. Be concise.

- Be upbeat and positive.

Be aware of your results. Do people respond well to your letter? If not, change it.

Sample Letter in Response to an Advertised Position

Rufus T. Firefly
1 Marx Place
Hollywood, California 90000
555-1212
Date_____

Mr. Irving Thalberg
Paramount Studios
Hollywood. California 90000

Dear Mr. Thalberg,

This is in response to your ad in the Wall Street Journal of December 31, 1937, for the position of madcap comedian. I believe my background is a very close match with your needs.

Your requirement	My qualifications
Five plus years of film experience	Over ten years of experience in movies such as Night at the Opera and Coconuts
Proven record of profit	Have grossed over $15,000,000
Expertise in writing	Have written scripts for six successful movies
Own your own funny clothing	Own over 75 ill-fitting suits

I look forward to meeting with you in the near future to discuss how I can contribute to your studio's success.

Sincerely yours,

Rufus T. Firefly

Recruiters/Employment Agencies

Recruiters (sometimes referred to as headhunters) and employment agencies serve as a go-between for organizations that have determined that they want to out source at least part of the process of hiring new talent.

They represent and are paid by the employer. Their loyalty is to the employer, then the job seeker.

Good recruiters know that the best outcome is a win-win, pleasing employer and candidate alike. The person they place may someday need to hire through a recruiter or be a useful contact to help the recruiter fill future jobs.

Recruiters usually want to place a square peg in a square hole. They would rather work with someone who is not trying to change industries or job functions because it's generally easier to present a candidate for a position who has already proven their ability to successfully carry out the functions of the job. If you want a recruiter to work with you, you need to make yourself into an attractive candidate, creating the right image and demonstrating how you can meet the employer's needs.

Recruiters are different from career counseling/marketing firms that counsel and market people who are looking for employment (and who charge their clients a fee for service). While some recruiters may help a client whom they see as having high potential, that is not what the job seeker should expect.

A recruiter should not request a fee from a job seeker, and you should be wary of anyone who does. In fact, avoid any recruiter who asks you for a fee.

Employment agencies that place full time employees tend to work with people earning less than $50,000 per year. Generally, these are hourly employees. The employment agency receives its fee after the employee has held their position for some contracted period of time.

Generally, you should have several agencies working on your behalf. Some agencies will tell you that they want to represent you on an exclusive basis. While that may be good for them, it does not help you.

After you send your resume to an employment agency, make sure that you call them to see who is going to be assigned to helping you. Make sure that you feel that they get to know you and your strengths. Be proactive in this process. Set up a meeting with them. If you get put off, don't consider them on your team.

Also, be aware that not everyone is equally good at his or her job or acts in an ethical manner.

More than once I have had clients asked about their job search, including specific places they have applied for work, and later found out that the company was contacted to see if they would be interested in other clients the employment agency represented.

Over the past several years, many agencies have expanded their focus to also include management and executive level employees, generally to work on specific, time limited projects.

How Recruiters are Paid

Recruiters are paid either on a retainer basis (an ongoing or up-front fee) for finding the right client or on a contingency basis (where they are paid only after the client organization has chosen to hire the candidate presented by the search firm).

Since search firms are looking for the ideal match, it is rare that they will present someone to an employer who isn't a very good fit. They don't want to "go out of the box."

The fees that recruiters get usually range from 25% to 35% of a person's salary. They usually work with positions that earn more than $40,000. Most retained searches are over $75,000.

If you use recruiters in your search, remember that you must stay in charge of staying in contact and being clear about what you want. Get several that will represent you. Remember, you must take responsibility for following up.

You should consider networking into recruiting firms, as well as using the *Directory of Executive Search*, the *Internet* and the *Yellow Pages* career websites to get leads. Ask people in different organizations which recruiters they use and trust.

Be aware that there are many more recruiting firms /employment agencies than there are good ones. I once researched local recruiters for one of my clients and found that over half the companies listed in the *Yellow Pages* were out of business. Those listings were less than a year old.

A good recruiter should help you prepare for an interview by giving you background data about the organization and the people that you meet for interviews. They will know the history of the position and of problems in filling it or retaining people in the past.

When it comes time to negotiate, try to do most of it yourself. Use the recruiter for gathering information and industry standards.

Remember who is paying the recruiters' fee.

Useful Career/Job Related Websites

The Internet is a very useful method to help find job leads and information about organizations. It allows you to research into an organization's history, provide you with up-to-date news, and lists you information about the competition. Many organizations put their job leads on their home page and skip the classified ads. If you are targeting organizations that you want to work for, you can't afford to overlook a company's website.

If you don't own a computer or updated smart phone, or similar device, you can generally get access to one through a local library or the state Department of Employment. In addition to company home pages, many associations list positions for their members. This can be a convenient way of finding what positions are open in a given specialization or geographic area. Various government agencies post positions they are advertising, and the department of labor in each state lists jobs sent to them by employers in each state. The type of job listed can range from an entry-level position to higher paying management and technical positions.

It is important to use the Internet wisely. It can be easy to get lost in the massive amount of data available, lose focus, or got distracted by news stories and social media, wasting hours of time. I have had clients who turned a useful tool into a time-consuming hobby or worse, an avoidance of more personal contact. Beyond research, using the Internet to search adds is a relatively passive job search method. It seldom develops synergy and has the disadvantage of putting you in competition with a large number of other, faceless individuals.

Fortunately, many websites provide access between employers and potential employees (even providing resume development), and the number seems to be getting larger by the day. These sites both list jobs and allow you to post information about yourself to be seen by employers using their services. When using one of the job search web sites, you have to be careful to follow directions exactly. Otherwise, you will have to spend time going over various forms several times. You also need to think through how you word your resume given that you will be screened by "keywords" that employers have determined will get them the right employee.

A good source for useful Internet Web Sites is *The Guide to Internet Job Searching;* Margaret Riley Dikel and Frances E. Roehm.

The following sites are among the many that are helpful:

America's Job Bank-http://www.ajb.dni.us

- Large national database of employment opportunities

Beyond.com

CareerBuilder-http://www.CareerBuilder.com

- National database of jobs

Career Magazine-http://www.careermag.com

- Job search by location, job skills and title. Also includes employer profiles and resume bank

Career Mosaic- http://www.careermosaic.com

- Large database of job opportunities

Career Path-http://www.careerpath.com

- Database of job opportunities featured in large newspapers around the country

Career Resource Center-http://www.careers.org

CareerWeb-http://www.cweb.com

- Search job databases

E-Span-http://www.espan.com

FlipDog.com

- A large job search site

Hoover's Company Search-http://www.hoovers.com

- Information about public and private companies

HotJobs-http://www.hotjobs.com

Indeed.com

- Aggregates a wide section of other sites

Job.com

JobTrak-http//www.jobtrak.com/profiles

- Provides links to home pages of organizations

NationJob Network-http://www.nationjob.com

* Job search by location, salary, fields of interests and education

Occupational Outlook Handbook-http://stats.bis.gov/ocohome.htm

* Find information about employers

Linkedin www.linkedin.com/

* Rapidly becoming one of the most important business networking sites

Monster.com-http://www.monster.com

* A very large site with dated listings

NJCAN - New Jersey Career Assistance Navigator

* https://njcis.intocareers.org/materials/portal/home.html

Snagajob.com

* All around job board

The Ladders

* Executive and professional positions

Yahoo! Employment-http://yahoo.com/business/employment/

* Has links to more than 1000 job sites

States and larger cities maintain their own Web Sites for employment opportunities. In addition, many organizations and industries list available jobs in their specialization.

Networking -

(Network or not work)

To be effective in a job search you need to be aware of how to access the most important resources. Since networking produces somewhere between 65% and 75% of all jobs, people are your most important resource. Networking is more than just knowing people; it's building alliances and creating win-win relationships. Whom you talk to should include family, friends, members of your community, and business relationships.

While the ultimate purpose of networking is to get in contact with people who can make the decision to hire you,you should also consider the opportunities for gathering information about various occupations and industries (informational interviewing). You may discover great job opportunities in professions or organizations that you haven't considered before. Especially when you are thinking about trying something new, you should talk to people who are experienced in that field.

Of the dozens of people interviewed for this book, almost all said that networking was the single most important method of getting a job. Even those who said that when they hire for their own organization they do so through ads admitted:

- People often found out about the ads through an acquaintance,
- The responses they received were sometimes accompanied by a recommendation from a mutual contact, or
- They themselves got their present job through a networking lead.

Carol Hyatt, author of *Switching Gears,* has stated that the average person knows 440 people. While you may not know that many people, you may be surprised at how many you do know when you create your own list of personal and business contacts.

Call 50 people you know. The goal is to get 3 leads from each person.

If you started with only 50 contacts and got three networking leads from each you would have 50 X 3= 150

150 and then made three contacts with each of them 150 X 3= 450 and then made three contacts with each of them 450 X 3= 1,350

6 Degrees of Separation

In John Guerre's play, *6 Degrees of Separation*, the premise is that every person is separated from any other person by no more than 6 linkages (someone who you know knows someone who knows someone, etc.).

Now, some contacts have better connections than others, but anyone is free to initiate a new relationship. Generally it is easier to leverage a relationship by using your contact's name when you introduce yourself. If you want to get your potential employer to accept your call, invoking your contact's name is more effective than making a cold call. That does not prevent you from calling the mayor of your city, or your senator, to develop job leads.

> *I counseled a Viet Nam vet who had trouble keeping employment. We (I wrote and he signed the letter) sent a letter to a U.S. Senator requesting help in getting employment. The Senator's Office called the client and provided an introduction that led to a much better paying job than he had before.*

One of the people interviewed for this book said that he had not actually conducted an active job campaign before he took his current position, then Executive Vice President, now President, of a major corporation. He believed that networking was a constant activity, that you were always developing and maintaining relationships. In taking this approach people were well aware of his activities and sought him out when an opportunity developed. This proactive, ongoing networking approach provides great rewards for those who follow it.

Getting Energized

Another positive aspect of networking is the interaction it provides you with others. In most cases people feel energized by positive feedback. I worked with a health care manager who was feeling down after leaving her job. She was not sure how marketable she was because she was over 55. Her willingness to talk to others provided her with a great deal of positive feedback. She learned of new opportunities and generated several interviews. Her biggest problem became sorting out multiple job offers.

Picture yourself in the middle of a web. You have access to people all around you; and you have access to the people that your contacts know as well, as long as you ask.

When I was growing up (in beautiful Newark, New Jersey), it was common for people to sit on their stoops at the end of the day. People would talk to each other and know what was going on with their neighbors. If someone needed a job, possibilities were often suggested by people you knew: "My cousin works at such and such a store, and I think they are hiring. Why don't you call him?" Nowadays, you may have to put in a little more effort to get equivalent results. You should make phone calls, go to professional and civic meetings, and write to contacts.

Going Beyond Your Resume

Here is an example of how networking works:

> *Janice wanted to return home to the state where she grew up and worked as a teacher. She had left the state, Kansas, years before and wasn't sure of the usefulness of her contacts anymore. Through conversations with her mother's bridge partner's daughter and a friend from high school she was able to get her resume hand carried to the Human Resources Office of the state Department of Education. She was subsequently interviewed and hired for a job that met all her requirements.*

Networking provides an opportunity to go beyond what your resume says about your qualifications:

> *Peter is a client whom I have worked with, off and on, for a couple of years. Initially, he wanted to leave the entertainment industry but was unclear about what he wanted to do next. While his assessment provided several new options, he felt uncomfortable regarding marketing himself. Once he had the opportunity to talk with networking contacts, his skills in communicating and persuasion opened up doors that led to his getting a sales position.*
>
> *Flash forward two years.*
>
> > *Peter was a top producer in his office, but due to a change in the economy and his company's policies he was somewhat limited in his income potential. In speaking with some of his contacts he was told that the industry he was targeting would only hire people who already had a track record in that industry. Another one of Peter's strengths is persistence. With my encouragement, he continued speaking to people about making the move to a new industry. He spoke about his sales ability and promoted his record of being able to make successful transitions. By creating an opportunity to have personal contact with decision makers, he was eventually able to create an opening for an interview. Persuasion and persistence led to a new job with much greater income potential.*

The Tipping Point

Malcolm Gladwell, in *The Tipping Point*, explains the way many situations get to the point where there is an exponential change in the behavior of people. He borrows the term "tipping point" from epidemiologists who use the term to describe the sudden, rapid spread of a disease to the point where it is considered an epidemic. I believe that successful networking needs to reach a "tipping point." You need to reach out to a lot of people to create the energy to get results. At first, the going may be slow, but if you persist, you will reach that tipping point where one contact leads to another, and another, and another. When you are successful at talking to several new people a day, you are well on your way to getting your new position.

You should start with a strategy regarding gathering information. How are you going to present what you want to do? What would you like to come away with from the discussion? Be open to suggestions and be flexible. If you have more than one possible career goal, consider if you want to address this with your contact. In some situations, you will focus on a specific goal. In other cases, you can be more general. In a networking meeting, you need to be clear about the help you want. If you are unclear, the contact will get confused and will be less helpful. In most cases people have limited time to talk to you. Don't forget being social but also get to the point.

Go Fishing

List brief reasons why you have targeted a particular career, industry or company. If your contact (the person you are talking to) is someone you were referred to (not someone you know directly), make reference to whoever introduced you. Show interest in the contact's background. He or she might have done what you want to do now. Ask how your contact got to his or her present position or situation. What worked for others might work for you. Show your contact your resume and ask for feedback regarding how clearly have you stated your goal (s). Ask for suggestions to make it stronger. Share with the contact what you have done so far in your job search.

Ask "if you were in my position" or "if you wanted to get a position with _____, whom would you talk to". Take down the name, address, telephone number and possibly e-mail address.

Ask your contact the best way to contact the third party (including suggestions about time of day). Ask if it is all right to use the contact's name. It's courteous to ask, and having a name is the leverage you need to get the person to talk to you. Once you have gotten the information about the first lead, ask your contact to recommend anyone else they can think of who could help you find a job. Try to get as many leads as possible from someone who is willing to help.

Tracking Leads

Be careful to keep track of every lead you get. If you do this you will never run out of leads. While you need to get to decision makers eventually, you never know which contact will lead you to that person.

It might be an ex-coworker, a cousin, a member of your alumni association, or a friend of a friend. Sometimes people overlook great opportunities right in front of them. One client stated he could think of no one who could be helpful to him. It turned out his godfather owned a professional football team and was connected to hundreds of people.

I have had clients who have gotten job leads from the relative of a friend of their grandmother - it turned out that this person was an executive recruiter. Or, from the husband of the tennis partner of a client's wife-he worked at a company that was hiring. And, from the parent of a child who was the teammate of a client's child on a little league team - he owned a company that needed a new comptroller. Make sure that you follow up with whomever you talk to.

The Barber Connection

Another client found out that the CEO of a company he wanted to work for went to the same barber he used. He made an appointment to be there at the same time, in the next chair. He was able to start a conversation, set up an appointment and begin the process that led him to his next position.

Some people are uncomfortable with the process of networking. You may not like feeling needy or dependent, or you may be fearful of rejection. But remember, most people are happy to help if they can. Help them help you. Ask for advice or leads, not for a job. Generally, if someone knows of a possibility and you have made a good impression, they will tell you about it. Remember that networking works in two directions. Always offer to provide help to those who have helped you if they or someone they know would like to call on you. Reciprocity is a good thing; you will enjoy the feeling of being helpful.

As with all aspects of the job search, you should send a thank you note to whomever has been helpful to you. You should do this immediately after a useful contact and at the conclusion of your search. Not only is this polite but it also informs people about where you are now employed. They may want to tell you about another opportunity some day.

Answering Ads

Job ads appear in many places

- National newspapers
- Local newspapers
- Trade journals
- State employment services
- Company bulletin boards
- Unions
- The Internet

Here are some things you should know about answering ads:

- Most jobs are not filled through advertising
- Usually, newspaper or Internet ads have a very high response rate (often hundreds or even thousands of replies)
- Some ads are put in circulation to meet legal obligations (such as for EEOC compliance). The organization may have an internal candidate already picked out.
- Some advertisements are for positions that are already filled by the time the ad appears.
- Some advertisements are not real. They are placed by recruiters or employment agencies or as market tests.
- To make the most of job ads:
- See if you can network into the organization versus simply responding in writing. If you can, call before you write.
- Write a cover letter that specifically addresses the requirements of the position.
- Research the company, if possible; show understanding and address issues that go beyond what the typical applicant does.
- Remember to get to the point. Use a one-page cover letter.

Targeting Employers (in a positive way)

There are many sources of information regarding organizations. Networking and reading newspapers are an excellent place to start. Do informational interviews (meeting with knowledgeable people to gather information about an industry). If you can't network into an organization you can send a letter directly to the appropriate decision-maker expressing interest, stating qualifications, and seeking a meeting. You can send such a letter with or without your resume. At worst, the decision-maker will tell you to follow the usual application process. Your cover letter can legitimately state that the decision maker recommended you apply.

- Check the organization's websites.
- Explore Industry Associations
- Contact Chambers of Commerce
- Read annual reports
- Use Linkedin
- Read the Business Section of your significant newspapers

Your local library will contain many of the following:

- Thomas Register of American Manufacturers
- Moody's Manuals
- Standard & Poor's Register of Corporations, Directors and Executives
- Dun & Bradstreet Million Dollar Directory
- America's Corporate Families
- Hoover's Handbook of American Companies
- Macmillan Directory of Leading Private Companies
- Directory of Directories
- Encyclopedia of Associations
- Macrae's Industrial Directories
- Consultants and Consulting Organizational Directory
- Ward's Directory of 49,000 Private U.S. Companies
- Ward's Directory of 51,000 Largest U.S. Corporations

Looking and Sounding the Part

How you look and sound to people will have a strong effect on how they view you for employment. Assume that during the job search (and other times as well) that any contact you have with people influences their impression of you. While many people know how to present themselves in appearance and communication with others, for those of you not totally sure, here are some reminders.

Appearance

Try to make the best impression you can. When you are meeting people for a networking meeting or interview, dress as well as the person you will be meeting.

While you are probably not going to be guilty of the following, do not:

- Dress like you are going to the gym (unless you are applying for the position of personal trainer),

- Dress like you are going to the prom or a nightclub, wear fatigues, dress like a member of the queen's entourage, wear out of the closet from twenty years, (or twenty pounds) ago.

- Never dress in the dark (I have known someone who had one black and one brown sock, and another pair just like it at home).

- If you are color blind or have no sense of fashion, get help from a friend with a good fashion sense.

- Look through magazines of better stores.

- How do the models dress who wear business clothes? Get advice from a knowledgeable sales person.

- Think about how political or business leaders dress. In general, choose conservative clothes and colors.

- In personal grooming, you should be consistent with your clothing. Forgive me if you think the following is unnecessary. Unfortunately, some people need a reminder. Always shower before a meeting.

- Use deodorant. If you use cologne, use it sparingly.

- Make sure your hair is properly groomed. Once again, conservative.

- If you color your hair, avoid primary colors and keep your roots the same color as the rest of it. Gents, avoid comb overs.

- Unless you are applying for the position of pirate, no earrings for men.
- No ankle jewelry, especially for men.
- Don't appear for an interview with sharp objects stuck through your face.
- Shine your shoes.
- Avoid wearing sunglasses indoors (unless your films gross over $100 million).
- Don't smoke before or during the interview.
- Don't eat garlic, onions or other odoriferous foods before the interview.
- Brush your teeth (spinach stuck on your teeth is generally unappealing).
- Don't chew gum during an interview; it's distracting.

First Impressions

Here is an exercise to help you prepare for an interview. You are going to do a short (two to three minutes) presentation as if you were at an interview. You are going to answer the prompt, "Tell me about yourself." Take a few minutes to think about what you want to say.

I suggest that you write down your response and then practice saying it while looking at yourself in a mirror. You want to emphasize pertinent education and employment history. Generally, you will begin at education and training; then give a chronological overview (past to present) with emphasis on the most recent work. If you are changing directions, emphasize your experience that supports your goal.

After your presentation what impressions do you think you made on the listener? Try giving your presentation to a trusted friend. Ask for his or her honest reaction. You are more likely to elicit a helpful response if you ask what part of your presentation was strongest and what part could be improved. Now, revise your presentation, and give it again. Practice, practice, practice. This is one of the most important rehearsals of your professional life.

Demonstrating Positive Work Attitudes

One of the things that employers say is most important to them is having employees with a good attitude. The following are some of the behaviors that go into having a good attitude. No matter how experienced a person is, the following are useful habits to develop, maintain, and communicate. During the course of an interview (or any communication), you should be aware of these guidelines.

- Start with the "golden rule."
- Be flexible.
- Demonstrate initiative.
- Demonstrate confidence.

- Maintain patience.
- Exhibit dependability.
- Exhibit honesty and integrity.
- Maintain confidentiality.
- Control emotions.
- Demonstrate a willingness to learn.
- Demonstrate an understanding of the company's culture and work environment.
- Exhibit pride in your work.
- Demonstrate loyalty to the employer.
- Do not criticize people behind their back.

Standard Interview Questions

Take this opportunity to think about how you want to answer these questions. In general, display characteristics of having a good attitude and use concrete examples of accomplishments when possible. Make sure you listen to the question, and answer the question asked.

Remember: The person interviewing you may be an accomplished interviewer or have little training in interviewing and be nervous themselves. Have patience and be helpful.

While questions regarding age, sex, religion, marital status, children and ethnic background may be illegal, don't be shocked if a poorly trained interviewer asks. Don't be argumentative if they do. Simply say something like, "I don't mind answering those questions, but are they relevant to my job performance?" Of course, if you do mind answering those questions, politely reply that you'd prefer to keep your personal life separate from your work life.

This is an opportunity to jot down some notes to prepare for these questions. While you will never be asked all of these questions your preparation will lead to a greater sense of confidence and clarity.

- Tell me about yourself. (focus on relevant education and work history)
- Why did you leave your last employer?
- What are your strengths?
- What are your weaknesses?
- What are your greatest accomplishments? (You should be able to discuss at least three and explain why you chose them)
- Describe your previous jobs.
- What is your ideal job? (Don't say you want the interviewer's or boss's position, even if you do. The timing is wrong.)
- Why did you choose this occupation? (Relate your answer to your strengths)
- Why do you want to work here?
- What are your long-term goals? (They should be tied in to first doing well in the position you are applying for)
- What is the most difficult situation you have handled, what did you do about it, and what was the outcome?

- What do you know about our organization? (You should have done some basic research.)

- Can you work nights/weekends? (If a managerial position, this will be considered a given. Make sure that your various life roles and goals can be balanced with the demands of the job)

- What are your salary expectations? (Once again, you should have done enough research to have an idea of what they are willing to pay.)

- Are you willing to travel?

- Would you be willing to relocate? (How will this affect you and your family, your spouse's career, and your children's education?)

- Why should I hire you? (Relate this to your strengths.)

- Where do you expect to be 5 (10) years from now?

- If you had to do it (or your life) all over again, what would you do differently?

- How do you feel about psychological tests? (They are fine)

- How have you resolved problems with your boss, peers, and subordinates? (Give win-win results.)

- Do you prefer to work alone or as part of a team? (The greater your flexibility the better. Give examples.)

- Have you ever been fired from a job or been asked to resign?

- What are you currently making? (You can choose salary or total compensation.)

- Describe a typical workday.

- How do you cope with stress? (Give an example of how you effectively deal with stress.)

- Can you give me 3 references? (You should be ready with their names, addresses, and telephone numbers.)

- Why were you out of work so long? (If you have been unemployed for an extended period you should have a good reason, one that doesn't damage your reputation. Don't blame others.)

- Why have you changed jobs so frequently? (Be prepared with good reasons such as growth, income, etc. Downsizing is appropriate – to a point).

- For Technical positions, be prepared for "what–if" questions. What if _____; what would you do? (Review major technical issues that you might need to deal with before the interview).

The following are sample, generic questions relevant to hiring a manager.

- How long have you been a manager?

- What led to your last promotion?

- How would you describe the job of a manager?

- How many people reported directly to you?

- Tell me about your experience hiring people?

- What are the factors most important to success in hiring?

- How much turnover occurred in your department in the last__ years? What were the circumstances?

- What are the steps you use in orienting new hires?

- Tell me about situations where you had to terminate an employee (s).

- How do you keep your staff aware of information and organization activities that might affect them?

- Describe your leadership style (How much do you involve other people? How do you do that?)

- How do you determine to whom and what you delegate?

- How do you motivate staff?

- Tell me about some of the conflicts you have had to deal with? What were the outcomes?

- Tell me about a time where you had to change an activity you were committed to because of a last-minute emergency. What did you do?

- How do you perform performance appraisals?

- What has been your budgetary responsibility?

- What kinds of problems have you had staying within budget? (Hopefully. few or none.)

- What are some of the important decisions you are called on to make?

- When faced with a difficult problem, how do you decide on what to do?

- Is there anything that you think is unique in the way you analyze problems?

- What do you think are the most significant issues affecting productivity?

- How would you go about improving worker productivity?

- Tell me about a particularly difficult problem you have had to face in your current position? What made this so difficult for you?

- Tell me about a recent experience in which your point of view differed from others? (Avoid sounding argumentative.)

- When several points of view have been developed, what process do you go through when evaluating alternatives?

- What are your goals regarding your professional career development?

- What do you see as your next step regarding your career development? (Similar to above question.)

- Do you have a personal mission or purpose statement? (If you have done the exercises in this workbook, you do.)

- How do you keep balance in your life?

- What did you learn about our organization before the interview?

- What kind of boss brings out the best in you?

- Who was the worst boss you ever had? What kinds of problems did you have with them? (Be careful about blaming)

- If we hired you for this position, what would be the first steps you can take? (Think before you respond)

- Tell me what process you have used in the past to meet your goals?

- Tell me about what you consider your greatest weaknesses? How do you compensate for them? (Consider a strength that may occasionally go too far -you get impatient with a lack of effort or a lack of experience that you have or are working on.)

- Can you give me some examples of your flexibility?

- Tell me about how you gain consensus?

- Tell me about how you deal with resistance to your ideas?

- Tell me about a time when not taking action turned out to work out for the best?

- Tell me about a situation when you had to make a quick decision.

- How do you manage your time?

- Can you think of a situation that you wish you had handled differently? What would you do now that would be different? Why?

- What are the most difficult issues in managing a schedule?

- How do you manage interruptions when you are working on an important task?

- What role(s) do you like taking when you work as part of a team?

- Describe your communication style?
- How do you make sure that a project is completed on time?
- If you had to choose between getting a project done on time and getting it done in a thorough way, which would you choose?
- Would you rather juggle a number of tasks or concentrate on one at a time?
- Do you prefer work on the "big picture" or the details of a project?
- Tell me about some of the presentations you have made. How have you prepared for them? Is this something you would like to do more of?
- Tell me about the best presentation you have ever made.
- Tell me about a time where you were able to change the actions of a group. How did you do it?
- Tell me about how you provide mentoring.
- How many of your subordinates have been promoted?
- What is the single biggest lesson that you can teach a subordinate?
- Who have been your mentors? How have they been of help to you?
- What kind of people do you enjoy mentoring the most?
- What kind of people do you have the most difficulty mentoring?
- What do you see as your strengths as a negotiator?
- What was the toughest group of employees that you have ever worked with? How did you handle the conflicts in the group?
- Tell me about a time that you negotiated a "win-win" situation.
- When have you had to compromise on an important situation? What was the outcome?
- How far would you go to please a client? colleague? boss? subordinate?
- Have there been times when you were not successful? How did you handle it?
- What is the most challenging aspect of entering a new work group?
- Do you see yourself as more of an introvert or extrovert? Why?
- How do people act to get on your good side?
- Tell me about a situation where you disagreed with an idea and were eventually persuaded to another point of view? How were you convinced?
- Who are the most difficult people for you to get along with? What do you do about it?
- What is the most effective way to get a group to cooperate?

- Have you ever changed your mind because your subordinates disagreed with you? (This is a measure of flexibility and openness.)
- Have you ever gotten angry at work? How did you handle it?

Identifying Position Objectives

Instructions: This form is designed to help you identify key tasks and functions of a job or position that you want (or intend) to hold in the future.

First, complete the information on the position and the industry sector.

Career/Position Title	
Industry Sector	

The next step is to list from 5 to 10 major objectives that the position is designed to achieve. For example, one such example for a **Regional Sales Manager** position might be *Hiring new sales representatives*. Another might be *Managing the regional advertising budget* or *Handling senior accounts*.

Do this for the position you have in mind in the spaces below.

1
2
3
4
5
6
7
8
9
10

Do you see yourself as a good fit for the position as you understand it?

Job Profiling

To help you identify the key tasks and functions of a job or position, you need to place yourself as the hiring organization. Similar to the way an employer judges a candidate, you become the analyst to ensure a good fit.

Give careful consideration as to are they a good match for what you are looking for.

The following questionnaire describes *31 Specific Task Categories* you can use to describe activities involved in a broad, cross section of managerial/professional positions.

The 31 tasks are grouped under 7 *Major Task Category* headings.

The form is designed to help you identify the top 8-10 task categories that are most critical to achieving the objectives of the position.

Instructions: Keeping the *Position Objective* in mind, review each of the 31 task categories and place a check mark if it applies to the objectives you have outlined on the *Identifying Position Objectives* sheet on the previous page.

Review each task in step one and place a second check mark if you see the task category as important (Poor performance in the category would significantly affect performance of your objectives)

If more than 8-10 task categories have been checked as important (2 checks) review the list and add a third check to the most critical tasks (no more than10).

Rank these most critical tasks from 1 (most critical) to 10 (least critical)

Managing Tasks				
1. Planning Determining short term and long-term priorities, objectives, schedules; revising plans, adjusting policy.				
2. Implementing/Coordinating Organizing resources and administrating systems, arranging events, ensuring good coordination.				
3. Controlling / Directing Controlling the use of human and material resources, following up with people; establishing procedures, rules and regulations.				
4. Reviewing / Evaluating(Systems /Methods) Assessing feasibility, compliance; evaluating reports, alternatives, efficiency , numerical data, projects and design.				
Managing People				
1. Supervising/Directing Taking the chair; administering tests; giving instructions, taking control in an emergency;maintaining a physical presence.				
2. Appraising/Evaluating/Developing Appraising for recruitment, promotion; evaluating work, behavior, needs of clients; showing patience; conducting formal & on-the-job training.				
3. Motivating Understanding others; reassuring, gaining cooperation, getting others to do unappealing tasks; emphasizing objectives, building team spirit.				
4. Assisting/Caring Addressing or helping with the emotional, physical, psychological needs and problems or learning difficulties of others.				
5. Disciplining /Disputes/Grievances Giving warnings; maintaining work standards; listening, resolving handling disputes firmly, reducing tension.				
6. Counseling Providing helpful counseling regarding the personal, social, physical problems, behavior, job performance of others; advising about the future.				
7. Cooperating / Liaison Working with other organizations, departments, groups, committees outside of own work area; arranging collaboration on joint projects.				
Receiving Information				
1. Investigating/Observing /Searching Listening to arguments, evidence, claims, disputes; establishing proof, observing; searching for hidden crimes, goods, neglect.				
2. Taking Information from the Senses Listening to and understanding verbal, written instructions; making fine judgments of color, taste, texture, auditory discrimination.				

Thinking Creatively				
1. **Artistic/Creativity** Designing, creating; devising charts, diagrams, visual forms, presentations.				
2. **Problem Solving / Designing (Methods/Equipment/Systems)** Brainstorming; designing questionnaires, products, services, solutions to problems, research methods				
3. **Assessing / Evaluating** Critically examining information; logical evaluation; assessing probability, quality, objects, people, correct function, writing content, style.				
4. **Analyzing / Diagnosing** Analyzing written, numerical information, trends in data, geographical sites; diagnosing personality, physical disorders, social problems, processes, systems.				
5. **Integrating / Coding / Estimating** Preparing statistics, flow diagrams; summarizing information, editing; estimating risk, time, quantity, rate of progress.				
4. **Calculating** Using calculators, algebra, trigonometry, geometry; doing simple or complex quantitative operations; calculating without a machine. Using calculators, algebra, trigonometry, geometry; doing simple or complex quantitative operations; calculating without a machine.				
5. **Interpreting** Interpreting rules, laws, agreements, statistics; translating; artistic interpretation; speaking a foreign language.				
6. **Checking** Checking work completion, specifications, standards; detecting defects in objects; verifying accuracy, inspecting by eye.				
7. **Deciding** Making decisions on own initiative or in conjunction with others; ruling on procedure; handling time pressure, decisions affecting other people.				
8. **Learning/Researching** Keeping abreast of developments; researching new systems, methods; applying theory, developing hypotheses, methods				
Communicating				
1. **Influencing / Advising** Arguing a case, negotiating, defending a position; advising on courses of action, procedures, policies.				
2. **Presenting / Instructing / Briefing** Presenting lectures; reading a script, explaining theory,briefing on tasks				
3.**Informing / Discussing / Interviewing** Answering questions, dictating; giving constructive criticism, verbal reports; providing information; structured, unstructured interviewing				
4. **Writing / Administrating** Preparing proposals, legal documents, instructions, description, detailed records, formal correspondence, writing for public audiences.				

5. Representing / Selling Contacting customers, negotiating price, answering, making inquiries; dealing with new or established customers.				
6. Influencing/Advising Arguing a case, negotiating, defending a position; advising on courses of action, procedures, policies.				
7. Presenting/Instructing /Briefing Presenting lectures; reading a script, explaining theory,briefing on tasks				
8. Informing Discussing/Interviewing Answering questions, dictating; giving constructive criticism, verbal reports; providing information; structured, unstructured interviewing				
9. Writing / Administrating Preparing proposals, legal documents, instructions, description, detailed records, formal correspondence, writing for public audiences.				
10. Representing / Selling Contacting customers, negotiating price, answering, making inquiries; dealing with new or established customers.				
11. Public Relations Developing Relationships Maintaining PR, advising the public, officiating, public speaking, establishing networks; dealing with antagonistic, busy people.				
Physical Activities				
1.Performing Physical Tasks/Operating Vehicles Performing physical work, engaging in sports, games, exercises, physical coordination, controlling vehicles.				
2. Using Tools / Machinery Using computers, precision tools, electronic machines; examining, checking, using machinery, equipment, drafting instruments.				

Principles of Negotiating

When you receive a job offer, it's time to enter into the negotiation that will establish the terms of your employment. Follow these guidelines for a successful negotiation.

Think win-win.

- Just as you cultivated a win-win attitude during your job search, think win-win during your contract negotiation.
- Start with the idea that the best outcome is one where all parties feel they have were treated fairly.
- If you get more than the employer really wants to pay, the employer may well set expectations that are very hard to meet.
- If you accept much less than you think is fair, you will probably feel resentful and not feel committed to the organization.

Keep a positive frame of mind.

- Negotiating is a give and take process.
- Until you have really explored all options, it is premature to draw conclusions.
- Sometimes it is helpful to think of yourself as your own client.
- What kind of attitude do you think the employer will respond best to? Wouldn't it be better to say "X" than "Y"?

Be clear about what you want.

- Know the difference between what you want and what you need.
- For instance, you may want X, but Y would suffice, and perhaps you should expect to work within the organization a while before they reward you with X.

Do your homework.

- Learn about the industry, organization, and department.
- What are their policies regarding salary?
- What is the salary range for a position?
- You can find out such information from published sources and from contacts.

Seek to understand the employer's point of view.

- Use your skills in creating empathy.

- What are his or her constraining factors?

- Where does the employer have flexibility?

Maintain your own flexibility.

- If you can't get exactly what you want now, consider the opportunities for the future.

- Be creative and think of the long-term relationship--and the total package.

Issues to Consider in Negotiating

What an organization will negotiate will be determined by many factors including industry, level of position, geographic location, and size of organization and labor market. The following issues are among those that can sometimes be negotiated.

- Base salary
- Pension plans
- Bonuses
- Medical plans
- Life insurance
- Disability
- Annual physical
- Sick time
- Personal time
- Vacation
- Educational benefits
- Sign-on bonus
- Club memberships

- Company car
- Employee assistance programs
- Mortgage money
- Closing costs
- Short-term salary reviews
- Professional development time
- Training programs
- Stock options
- Profit sharing
- Severance
- Outplacement
- Product discounts
- Company purchase of home

Tracking Job Search Activities

An effective job search campaign needs to be monitored for both quality and quantity of activities. Unless one is very fortunate and gets an offer immediately (it happens, but don't count on it), treat the search as a full-time job.

Some people track their activities on their computer, others the old-fashioned way. Remember, you are looking for tangible results. Telephone calls that get busy signals or that do not result in speaking with your target don't get counted. In determining effectiveness, remember that face-to-face meetings are more productive than phone calls and phone calls more productive than letters or emails. Combine reasonable expectations with frequently monitoring your progress. Be honest and fair in evaluating your activities. Discuss with trusted advisors on how you are doing and be open to improvement. We learn as we search.

For the seven days ending:	
Number of ads answered	
Number of recruiters contacted	
Number of direct mail letters sent	
Number of applications completed	
Number of networking contacts	
Number of networking leads	
Number of informational interviews	
Number of job interviews	

Job Offers - Criteria for Chosing a Job

To help you target the best job for you and to help you decide when you get an offer, please look at the job criteria on this page. Rate each of the criteria listed below as to their importance to you on a scale of 1 to 10 (10 being the highest).

Criteria	Job Offer A	Job Offer B	Job Offer C	Criteria	Job Offer A	Job Offer B	Job Offer C
Advancement opportunities				Autonomy			
Benefits				Challenge			
Childcare				Commuting distance			
Geographic location				Health			
Industry				Leisure time			
Mentor availability				Power and influence			
Prestige				Respect for co-workers			
Service orientation				Salary			
Security (apparent)				Size of organization			
Stress level				Title			
Travel							

Are you being Realistic?

The Unpredictable and the Irrational

During my career counseling experience, and in researching this book, I have encountered many situations and actions that were neither predictable nor especially rational regarding job search situations. While I encourage you to take responsibility for your own actions, it is important to know some situations exist that go beyond your control. You still need to make the best of the situation. Here are examples.

The people you expect to help you—don't.

Almost every individual I have ever worked with has encountered people who they thought would help in the job search and did not. You call your "friend" or colleague who does not respond at all or says, "I'll get back to you"-and never does. Why? In some cases, it can be because of an inadequate presentation as to how these individuals can help you. They think that anything less than a direct lead to a job is insufficient, so they feel embarrassed or put upon and then avoid you. Or, they are "work friends." These are people who are pleasant to deal with as long as you are a coworker, but as soon as circumstances change you never hear from them again. It is important to not get discouraged if a few people do not follow through.

Total strangers provide great help.

The good news is that you will encounter other people you barely knew who will be helpful and supportive, and some of these people may be real and lasting friends.

You never know who "they" know.

You seldom know everyone who is a friend or acquaintance of the people in your social or business circle or, you take whom you know for granted. It is important to explore all these possibilities during your job search.

People don't return your phone calls.

I once worked with a high-level executive who refused to contact any networking lead after not getting return phone calls. He thought it was futile and believed, now he was no longer president of a company, no one wanted to talk to him. One of the most frustrating parts of a job search is waiting for people to get back to you. First, remember that your need to move ahead in your job search will be greater than your contacts' need to get back to you. They may not share your urgency. In addition, many people feel overwhelmed by their responsibilities at work and don't want to be looking for a job themselves. It is safer to always suggest that you will take the responsibility to say when you will call to follow up. This puts your actions back in your own hands and may generate motivation by the person who knows they are going to hear from you again (soon). Remember, the nicer you are the harder you can push.

They said they would get back to you.

This goes farther than just getting a return phone call. You thought you had a great first (or second) interview and now are in limbo. What happened? Well, you could call and ask, but even then, you might not get an answer, or an answer that makes sense. One employer I interviewed told me of a situation where a female candidate who in other ways had made a good impression, was disqualified by an internal recruiter because she had worn the same clothing to two successive interviews. The interviews were over three weeks apart. The person being interviewed was being considered for a professional level position at a pharmaceutical company and probably did not remember what she had worn several weeks earlier. This one factor was so negative to the recruiter, and a viable candidate was disqualified on that basis alone. It is an unfortunate fact of life you may not always be treated fairly, or even reasonably.

I have worked with dozens of individuals who thought that they would receive an offer for a position and then heard nothing for months. Sometimes, they were eventually offered the position. In one instance, they delayed the position of President of a large hospital for almost a year because of an internal political conflict. In another, a recruiter contacted someone after 2 ½ years to inquire if the individual was still interested in a particular position (in the interim the individual had changed careers). Delays can take place because of financial problems, mergers and acquisitions, a change in company direction, an internal promotion or demotion, a transfer, or other circumstances that impact on you but are out of your control.

An interview goes inexplicably wrong.

Everyone has experienced an interview that, no matter how much you have prepared, has gone wrong. You and the other person just don't "click". There are many possible reasons for this, some of which you can correct, and some of which you can't. You may remind someone of a relative or acquaintance that they have problems with (they may not know of this connection). If you seem similar to a hated cousin, your chances of being hired are slim. In one situation, the job candidate picked up on the interviewer's seeming to relate in an inappropriate manner. He asked, in a gentle fashion, if he reminded the interviewer of anyone he knew. Luckily, the interviewer could see he were responding inappropriately because the applicant reminded him of an older brother with whom he felt competitive. The interview got back on track and they offered the individual the job.

In another situation, an individual waiting to be interviewed asked about the substantial delay in starting the interview (an hour). They eventually discovered that the interviewer was having a crisis in their family and was clearly upset. Under these circumstances it might be best to request another appointment at a later time. Not only are you being considerate but also are likely to have more of the interviewer's attention (who might want to make up for the delay).

A client who was very well qualified for a senior position was considered not serious enough because he told a joke (tasteful) during an interview.

What were they thinking?

Under a category that I will call "what were they thinking," I have had clients who were asked to come to an interview and then put through very stressful and not very well thought out circumstances. One client was flown by first class to Europe for what turned out to be a fifteen-minute face-to-face interview with the corporate CEO. They notified him of the decision (he was hired) when they arrived home. Another client was flown by private plane to company headquarters where he met a number of managers and technical people throughout the day. The day lasted from 7:30 A.M. until midnight. During the day, he was escorted wherever he went, from plane, to limousine, to a sequence of interviews and meetings, to lunch, dinner and bathroom breaks and back to the airport. It would be fair to say he was exhausted by the time he returned home. Another client went to New York City to meet with a recruiter. The meeting started at 4:00 P.M. and ended at midnight. While the client excused himself for bathroom breaks, there was no mention of such by the recruiter, or a break for food. Nothing came from this meeting.

Recently, a client went to an interview and was asked how she did her laundry. Perhaps the interviewer was seeking insight into how the job candidate organizes her activities.

While they generally see the *stress interview* as nonproductive and/or inappropriate, there are still those who use it. If you encounter it, you must show patience. A variation on this is the multiple interviewer process. Having 12 people ask you questions simultaneously can be daunting, especially since it is unlikely that the employer has carefully thought out the process or organized the questioning. In this situation, always make eye contact first with the person who asked the question. Then look at the other people in the room, especially the decision makers.

Other's Perspectives of Personal Attributes

(optional assessment)

This assessment provides feedback to individuals regarding their behavior and attitudes at work. It uses definitions from *Caliper Corporation*. With this information, they can compare your perception of them with the image that they have of themselves. Your perspective can provide a more balanced picture to them and identify possible blind spots that they have (both positive and negative). With a better sense of their job-related personal attributes, they will be in a stronger position to create a successful career-development plan.

Instructions: On the following pages, you are presented with a list of attributes that can be used to describe the ways people behave, think, and feel in different positions in different work settings. To the right of each of the attributes you will find a 10-point scale for rating how you see the person being rated. Below each of the attribute headings are phrases that describe someone who rates himself/herself high on the scale. Given your knowledge and experience of the person being rated, consider each attribute listed and rate on the 10-point scale the extent to which you feel the characteristics or qualities describe their typical behavior, or their usual reactions to people or situations. Use other managers and professionals as a context for rating and comparing them. Circle the one number on the scale that best reflects your sense of how they compare to other managers and professionals on the attribute.

	Low - - - - - - - - - - - - - - - -High
Persuasive	1 2 3 4 5 6 7 8 9 10
The innate need to persuade others as a means of gaining personal satisfaction. Individuals scoring high on persuasion will tend to seek other people's commitment for the sheer satisfaction of winning through persuasion	
Assertiveness	1 2 3 4 5 6 7 8 9 10
Assertiveness is the ability to express one's thoughts forcefully and consistently without having to rely on anger. Those with a low score on this characteristic are not comfortable communicating their ideas and opinions in a direct manner and tend to be more reluctant to confront issues.	
Aggressiveness	1 2 3 4 5 6 7 8 9 10
This is an emotion-based way of expressing oneself and tends to be more reactive tend proactive. Unlike assertiveness, individuals who have high aggressiveness may be "heavy-handed" in their approach in "getting their way". Some degree of aggressiveness can be valuable. Those with a low score may be uncomfortable when it comes to supporting a not readily accepted position.	
Resilience	1 2 3 4 5 6 7 8 9 10
Resilience is the ability to handle rejection and accept criticism in a manner which is constructive and growth oriented. People high in resilience tend to have a healthy, intact ego and a positive self-image. Those scoring low tend to be more self-critical and less tolerant of critical feedback and rejection.	
Urgency	1 2 3 4 5 6 7 8 9 10
Urgency is an inner-directed and focused need to get things done. Extremely high scores indicate impatience or unrealistic expectations. Low levels indicate patience or a potential for complacency.	
Risk Taking	1 2 3 4 5 6 7 8 9 10
This quality reflects the degree of comfort one has taking chances or trying new things. It does not imply recklessness (i.e.; one can be a calculated risk taker).People scoring high in this area may be intrigued by taking chances and trying new things. Those with a low score tend to prefer conventional or well-established methods.	
Empathy	1 2 3 4 5 6 7 8 9 10
Empathy is the ability to accurately sense the reactions of another person. People with high levels of empathy can "put themselves in the other person's shoes" (not necessarily agree with the other person).	
Cautiousness	1 2 3 4 5 6 7 8 9 10
This characteristic relates to the speed with which one is comfortable in making decisions. Very high rankings indicate the need to make decisions slowly.	

	Low - - - - - - - - - - - - - - - -High
Sociability	1 2 3 4 5 6 7 8 9 10
Sociability is defined as a need to seek out the company and camaraderie of others. Individuals who rank high in this quality enjoy being and working with others. Such individuals relate well in one-on-one situations. People who rank low are usually more comfortable when they are not expected to interface on a regular basis with a wide variety of people.	
Gregariousness	1 2 3 4 5 6 7 8 9 10
Gregariousness is extroverted, ebullient optimism. Gregarious people are outgoing and enjoy working with large groups; a genuine enjoyment of social interaction. Those scoring low in this area can be reserved and uncomfortable in new, unknown social situations.	
Accommodation	1 2 3 4 5 6 7 8 9 10
Individuals who have high scores in this dimension tend to be helpful and service oriented. They also have a need to be liked, respond to recognition and work hard to please others. Those scoring low do not feel a strong need to get approval.	
Skepticism	1 2 3 4 5 6 7 8 9 10
Skepticism is a doubting or questioning state of mind. Individuals scoring high in this quality tend to be suspicious of other's motivations. Low levels on this scale suggest possible naiveté.	
Self-Structure	1 2 3 4 5 6 7 8 9 10
Self-structure indicates a preference for determining one's own priorities and methods for managing tasks. People with high scores tend to be self-disciplined. They are able to coordinate multiple activities and typically are good at organizing activities. People with low scores may require help and direction when defining and setting priorities. They may be more comfortable in an environment where parameters and guidelines are established and communicated.	
External-Structure	1 2 3 4 5 6 7 8 9 10
Individuals scoring high in external structure are sensitive to externally-defined rules, policies and procedures. They operate with some sensitivity to authority and will generally prefer a working environment in which direction is set.	
Conscientiousness	1 2 3 4 5 6 7 8 9 10
Conscientiousness is a willingness to be thorough and responsible in completing tasks and assignments. Those with a high score tend to display a strong commitment to upholding high quality standards. A low score can show restlessness with details and distractability. Individuals with low scores can become easily bored with routine.	

Low - - - - - - - - - - - - - - - -High									
Insight 1 2 3 4 5 6 7 8 9 10									
High insight scores indicate the ability to perceive situations with accuracy. The individual high in insight demonstrates a high level of understanding.									
Energy 1 2 3 4 5 6 7 8 9 10									
This is in reference to psychological energy. Individuals with high-energy scores tend to want to do many things on a given day, are able to move from task to task without tiring and quite willing to do hard work. There are several possible reasons for a low energy score including personal distractions.									
Openness 1 2 3 4 5 6 7 8 9 10									
People high in openness are open-minded and perceive different points of view. Individuals low in openness avoid ideas different from those they already hold.									
Abstract Reasoning 1 2 3 4 5 6 7 8 9 10									
Those with high levels tend to be somewhat more expansive in their ability to handle complex or multi-dimensional problems. Those with lower levels tend to be more concrete.									
Idea Orientation 1 2 3 4 5 6 7 8 9 10									
Individual with high scores show an orientation To be creative in area of problem solving, idea generation and concept development. Lower scores may indicate a preference for practical or concrete solutions.									
Flexibility 1 2 3 4 5 6 7 8 9 10									
Individuals who rank high in this quality are generally willing to modify their approach as changing conditions and circumstances require. Those with lower scores are more tenacious in holding to their views and less willing to modify their positions.									
Confidence 1 2 3 4 5 6 7 8 9 10									
Confidence is the courage, self-worth and comfort one brings to social, problem-solving and leadership situations. High scores indicate a good self-concept and esteem; low scores indicate a reduced sense of self-evaluation and worth.									
Anxiety 1 2 3 4 5 6 7 8 9 10									
The individual with high anxiety tends to be tense, worried and easily upset. They find it upsetting to function under pressure and don't believe in themselves. Individuals with low anxiety tend to be calm, resilient with respect to failure and are able to face new situations without worry.									

Development Plan

Compare the results from the various assessment instruments you have used to understand your strengths and weaknesses. Next, describe your goals for the kind of life you wish to live and the kind of job you wish to have. Where would change/improvement have the greatest positive impact? Pick three areas that you would like to work on and write a brief plan for improvement for each. The more specific you are as far as concrete goals the more likely you will make it happen.

About the Author

Larry Finkelstein is Founder and President of Transition Management Associates (TMA), a Human Resource Consulting firm headquartered in Lambertville, New Jersey. TMA provides Outplacement Consulting to corporate clients and coaches individuals who are seeking employment. As President of TMA, Larry has worked with hundreds of people looking for career help, at all levels (hourly employees to CEO's) and stages (from students through retirement age). Larry has consulted to Fortune 500 organizations, small and medium sized businesses, Workforce Investment Boards/JTPA's, high school and college students, welfare clients and people who are transitioning to retirement. TMA has provided consulting in Career Development and Mentoring to the New Jersey State Departments of Labor, Education and State, The New Jersey Business and Industry Association, The New Jersey Food Council many Chambers of Commerce and several national associations. Larry has provided Retirement Planning to organization as diverse as GM, Dow Chemical, numerous school systems and hospitals.

Prior to TMA, Larry worked as a Vice President at Right Associates, the world's largest career transition firm. Earlier career related coaching was done at Minsuk Macklin Stein and Drake Beam Morin.

Simultaneously, Larry is a licensed psychotherapist. In what now seems like a lifetime ago he worked for Rutgers Medical School and Beth Israel Medical Center in New Jersey.

Larry has been certified in a number of career assessment instruments such as the Caliper, Occupational Personality Questionnaire, LifeStyles Inventory, Strong Interest Inventory, Myers Briggs Type Indicator and others. In addition, he was certified as a trainer for the Covey Leadership Institute.

Larry holds a MA Ed. In Counseling from Seton Hall University and a BA in Political Science from Rutgers University.

Larry grew up in Newark, New Jersey but now lives in Lambertville, New Jersey, with his two collies, Cola and Barbie, and runs a large Meet-up Group.

Acknowledgements

Many people have contributed to the completing of this book. I want to thank:

- my clients who provided me with real life feedback as to what worked for them, and what didn't. It is from their experience that most of this book is drawn.

- the many employers who agreed to be interviewed regarding their process for hiring and sharing their own career experiences.

- my many career counseling colleagues who shared their knowledge and experiences with me. In this regard, special thanks to Denise Higgins, who worked with me, off and on, for 25 years.

Contributing to the writing, editing and making useful suggestions that took my idea to a published book include:

- **Vincent Miskell** teaches psychology and sociology courses at Johnson & Wales University in South Florida. His undergraduate degree is from Rutgers University (where he became friends with Larry). His master's degree is from Empire State College (SUNY), and he's earned doctoral credits in counseling psychology. He provided line by line feedback, on content and style (and made it clear that I used too many words). He is the co-author (along with his wife Jane) of *Overcoming Anxiety at Work* and *Motivation at Work*.

- **Dr. Beverly Petersen,** Associate Professor of English, Emerita Penn State Fayette. I have been friends with her for 30 years. She provided early feedback and structure. She, and her husband, Dr. Joseph Galano, have been discussing this work with me, since we first met.

- **Elise Marton** is a freelance editor with a long career in Manhattan-based consumer magazines; today she specializes in books and web content, now that print journalism is all but dead. She has lived in just about every city on Amtrak's Northeast Corridor, including Boston, Providence, Stamford, New York, Princeton, and Philadelphia. She has her eye on the Orient Express next.

- **Jeanne Johansen** at High Tide Publications, Inc. who provided wise, patient advice in the formatting, editing, and production of my book.

Appendix

Suggested Reading List

Angel, Juvenal L. (1980) *The Complete Resume Book & Job-Getter's Guide*. New York, Pocket books.

Barker, Joel Arthur. (1993) *Paradigms*, New York, Harper Collins Publishers.

Beckhard, Richard and Pritchard, Wendy (1992). *Changing the Essence*. San Francisco, Jossey-Bass Inc.

Berne, Eric (1964). *Games People Play*. New York, NY Grove Press.

Berne, Eric (1975). *Transactional Analysis*. New York, Grove Press.

Block, Peter (1991). *The Empowered Manager*. San Francisco, Jossey-Bass.

Block, Peter (1993). *Stewardship*. San Francisco, Berrett-Koehler Publishers.

Bolles, Richard (1972). *What Color is Your Parachute?* Berkeley, California, Ten Speed Press.

Boldt, Laurence G (1993). *Zen and the Art of Making a Living*. New York, Penguin Books.

Bridges, William (2004) *Transitions - Making Sense of Life's Changes(25th anniversary edition)*. Da Capo Lifelong Books.

Bridges, William (1988). *Surviving Corporate Transitions*. New York, Doubleday.

Bridges, William (1995). *Jobshift: How to Prosper in a Workplace Without Jobs*. Da Capo Lifelong Books.

Bridges, William (2000). *The Character of Organizations: Using Personality Type in Organization Development*. Nicholas Brealey.

Briggs Myers, Isabel and Mary H. McCaulley (1985). *Manual: A Guide to the Development and Use of the*
Myers-Briggs Type Indicator. Consulting Psychologists Press.

Brown, Duane and Brooks, Linda (1984). *Career Choice and Development*, San Francisco, Jossey Bass.

Bry, Adelaide (1978).*Visualization*, New York, Harper and Row.

Caliper Human Strategies (2000). *The Caliper Hiring Manual*, Princeton, NJ.

Covey, Stephen R. (2013). *7 Habits of Highly Effective People: Powerful Lessons in Personal Change*. New York, Simon and Schuster; Anniversary edition.

Covey, Stephen R. (1992). *Principle-Centered Leadership*. Fireside Press; Reprint edition.

Covey, Stephen R. and Merrill, A. Roger, and Merrill, Rebecca R (1996). *First Things First*. Free Press; Reprint edition.

Ellis, Albert and Harper, Roger A. (1997). *A New Guide to Rational Living*. Wilshire Book Company.

Ellis, Albert and Dryden, Windy (1997). *The Practice of Rational Emotive Behavior Therapy*. Springer Pub co; second edition.

Evans, David R. and Hearn, Margaret T.and Uhlemann, Max r. and Ivey, Allen E. (2007). *Essential Interviewing: A Programmed Approach to Effective Communication*. Brooks Cole; eighth edition.

Farr, J. Michael and Ludden, LaVerne L (2011). *Best Jobs for the 21st Century (6th Edition)*. Indianapolis, Indiana, JIST Publications.

Farr, Michael and Shatkin, Laurence (2005). *50 Best Jobs for Your Personality*. Jist Works.

Gawande, Atul (2009). *The Checklist Manifesto*. New York, Henry Holt and Company.

Gardner, Howard (2006). *Changing Minds*. Boston, MA, Harvard Business School Press.

Gladwell, Malcolm (2000). *The Tipping Point*. New York, Little Brown & Company.

Gould, Richard (1986). *Sacked*. New York, John Wiley & Sons.

Gould, Roger L. (1978) *Transformations*. New York, Simon& Schuster.

Handy, Charles (1990). *The Age of Unreason*. Boston, MA Harvard Business School Press.

Holland, John L. and Messer, Melissa A. (2017). *Standard Self-Directed Search Technical Manual*. PAR, Inc.

Hyatt, Carole (1990). *Shifting Gears*. New York, Simon & Schuster.

Jaffe, Dennis T. and Scott, Cynthia (1988). *Take This Job and Love It: How to Change your Work without Changing your Job*. New York, Fireside Publishers.

Keirsey, David and Bates, Marilyn (1984). *Please Understand Me*. Carlsbad, CA, Prometheus Nemesis Book Company.

Kinlaw, Dennis (1995). *Coaching: The ASTD Trainer's Sourcebook*. New York, McGraw-Hill.

Kushner, Harold (1986). *When All You've Ever Wanted Isn't Enough*. New York, Summit Books.

McClelland, Carol (2010). *Green Careers for Dummies*. Hoboken, NJ Wiley Publishing Inc .

Morin, William J. and Yorks, Lyle (1982). *Outplacement Techniques*. New York, Professional Educational Materials.

Myers, Albert (1984). *Success Over 60*. New York, Summit Books.

Nierenberg, Gerard (1973). *Fundamentals of Negotiating*. New York, Harper and Row, Publishers .

Overholt, Miles H. *(1996). Building Flexible Organizations - A People-Centered Approach*. Dubuque, Iowa, Kendall/Hunt Publishing.

Peters, Tom (1999). *The Circle of Innovation. Vintage;* abridged edition.

Reardon, Kathleen (1996). *They Don't Get It, Do They?* New York, Little Brown & Co.

Ryan, Kathleen D. and Oestreich, Daniel K. (1998). *Driving Fear Out of the Workplace*. Jossey-Bass; second edition.

Seligmann, Martin (2011). *Flourish*. New York, Simon & Schuster.

Senge, Peter M. (1990) *The Fifth Discipline*. New York, Doubleday.

Schrank, Louise Welsh (1991). *How to Choose the Right Career*. Chicago, Ill, VGM Career

Horizons.

Tieger, Paul D. *Do What You Are: Discover the Perfect Career for You Through the Secrets of Personality Type.* (2014). Little, Brown Spark; fifth edition.

Tomasko, Robert (1989). *Downsizing: Reshaping the Corporation for the Future.* AMACOM/American Management Association; Expanded & Updated ed.

Weisbord, Marvin R. (1978). *Organizational Diagnosis: A Workbook of Theory and Practice.* Basic Books.

Yate, Martin (2017). *Knock 'Em Dead Holbrook,* MA, Adams Media Corporation, 2017

Yate, Martin (2016). *Resumes that Knock 'Em Dead.* Holbrook, MA Adams Media Corporation.

Reproducible Forms

Copies of the forms used in this book are are reproducible for personal use.

Tracking Job Search Activities

An effective job search campaign needs to be monitored for both quality and quantity of activities. Unless one is very fortunate and gets an offer immediately (it happens, but don't count on it), treat the search as a full-time job. Some people track their activities on their computer, others the old-fashioned way. Remember, you are looking for tangible results. Telephone calls that get busy signals or that do not result in speaking with your target don't get counted. In determining effectiveness, remember that face-to-face meetings are more productive than phone calls and phone calls more productive than letters or emails. Combine reasonable expectations with frequently monitoring your progress. Be honest and fair in evaluating your activities. Discuss with trusted advisors on how you are doing and be open to improvement. We learn as we search.

For the seven days ending:	
Number of ads answered	
Number of recruiters contacted	
Number of direct mail letters sent	
Number of applications completed	
Number of networking contacts	
Number of networking leads	
Number of informational interviews	
Number of job interviews	

Identifying Position Objectives

Instructions: This form is designed to help you identify key tasks and functions of a job or position that you want (or intend) to hold in the future.

First, complete the information on the position and the industry sector.

Career/Position Title	
Industry Sector	

The next step is to list from 5 to 10 major objectives that the position is designed to achieve. For example, one such example for a **Regional Sales Manager** position might be *Hiring new sales representatives*. Another might be *Managing the regional advertising budget* or *Handling senior accounts*.

Do this for the position you have in mind in the spaces below.

1	
2	
3	
4	
5	
6	
7	
8	
9	
10	

Do you see yourself as a good fit for the position as you understand it?

Reference Worksheet

Use this worksheet to list the confirmed information regarding your references. Make sure that you have up-to-date information. Always bring a typed copy of your references to an interview.

Title	Name	
Address		
City	State	ZIP
Telephone Numbers		
Email		
How do you know this individual?		
Title	Name	
Address		
City	State	ZIP
Telephone Numbers		
Email		

Title of Previous Position:
Dates of Employment:
What I Liked About the Position:
1.
2.
3.
4.
5.
What I Disliked About the Position:
1.
2.
3.
4.
5.

Title of Previous Position:
Dates of Employment:
What I Liked About the Position:
1.
2.
3.
4.
5.
What I Disliked About the Position:
1.
2.
3.
4.
5.

Perfect Work Environment

Think about what you would consider an ideal work environment. Develop work goals to determine what would make that environment a reality. Write down the specifics of:

Physical environment:
The characteristics of the work tasks:
The relationships among the personnel:
The benefits that you gain from the total work environment (money, benefits, training)
Any other factors or situations that you feel are important to the creation of an ideal work environment

Perfect Work Environment

Think about what you would consider an ideal work environment. Develop work goals to determine what would make that environment a reality. Write down the specifics of:

Physical environment:

The characteristics of the work tasks:

The relationships among the personnel:

The benefits that you gain from the total work environment (money, benefits, training)

Any other factors or situations that you feel are important to the creation of an ideal work environment

Index

Feedback

I would appreciate feedback on the effectiveness of this book in helping you find a new job/career. I would also like to hear about the methods you have found that work for you. Please use the contact form on www.LarryFinkelstein.org (http://larryfinkelstein.org/contact-us/)

If you feel this book has been helpful, you can write a recommendation at Larry Finkelstein on Linkedin and Amazon.com

In your email, I would love to hear what you thought about the book:

1. What were the most valuable parts of the book?
2. What topics would you like to know more about?
3. What, if anything, would you change about this book?
4. What do you plan to do differently because of what you learned?

Thanks you.